TERTULIA

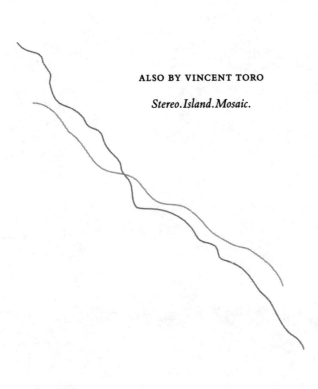

ALSO BY VINCENT TORO

Stereo.Island.Mosaic.

TERTULIA

VINCENT TORO

PENGUIN POETS

PENGUIN BOOKS
An imprint of Penguin Random House LLC
penguinrandomhouse.com

LIBRARY OF CONGRESS CATALOGING-IN-PUBLICATION DATA
Names: Toro, Vincent, 1975– author.
Title: Tertulia / Vincent Toro.
Description: [New York] : Penguin Books, [2020]
Identifiers: LCCN 2019044793 (print) | LCCN 2019044794 (ebook) |
ISBN 9780143135340 (paperback) | ISBN 9780525507000 (ebook)
Subjects: LCGFT: Poetry.
Classification: LCC PS3620.O5878 T47 2020 (print) |
LCC PS3620.O5878 (ebook) | DDC 811/.6—dc23
LC record available at https://lccn.loc.gov/2019044793
LC ebook record available at https://lccn.loc.gov/2019044794

Printed in the United States of America
1 3 5 7 9 10 8 6 4 2

Set in Bembo Book MT Std
Designed by Ginger Legato

For the discarded, the uprooted, the dissed,
the banned, the banished, the policed,
the scapegoated, the grief-stricken, the ghosted,
the abstracted, the unclaimed, the profiled,
the belittled, the bullied, the blamed,
the outcast, the sapped, the chided,
the denied, the distraught, the unwritten,
the misconstrued, the maimed, the muzzled,
the resilient, the defiant, the inflamed;
you know, the marvelous ones. In solidarity.

For Grisel, the Original Latina Outsider

CONTENTS

⇒ ACT THREE

⇒ ACT FOUR

→ ACT FIVE

A common ritual in Spain and Latin America, the tertulia is a salon or gathering typically held in someone's home. Tertulia attendees hold roundtable conversations on art, politics, science, philosophy, and current events, as well as participate in impromptu literary, musical, and dramatic performances. Tertulias serve as informal academy and social arena, a singular space where one can go to learn, to celebrate, and to organize community action.

ACT ONE

". . . in a cage sudden with blossom."

María Negroni

On Battling (Baltimore Strut)

Gray cased in gray, shaken
       and truncated like timber,
       the bleat rouses all provinces,
calling each seed to surface

and insist on a redress. This trumpet
       of grief and homespun placards
       is met with gunmetal treads
bruising the fruit stands, mustard

gas suffocating the night's
       coruscation. As elbows
       lock before storefronts
to shelter shop windows

from the wallop of pitiless
       Kevlar, as flares browbeat
       boulevards and arsenals
are dispatched across the wet

gravel, a single shirtless
       seraph unfurls himself
       upon the tarmac. Flexing
faux leather, he gyrates, feather-

glides, thunderclaps, then jukes
       toward the 16,000-pound
       armored personnel carrier.
The bullying smog flinches

at his voltaic gait, as he peacocks
       into the boomerang hour,
       cranes his neck and shrieks
to remind the intruder *your tanks*

are no match for my toprock.

➤ *Days of Being Wild* (dir. Wong Kar-Wai, 1990)

(Dissolve)

At the funeral of his birth the seamstresses sing matte-muted adagio
of rouge and torn hems. Oleaginous in both mane and vow. Bronze

king of ennui. She drifts across oxidized hallways. Her dress, the slug
line. Blue filtered lights and non-filtered cigarettes imbibe them.

> CUT TO: *Closing credits. Exit. Pressed*
> *suit preens for role*
> *as auteur's unsung enigma.*

One mistakes soliloquy for an affair. The other lives as an atoll, divot-
headed and bleak-lacquered. Boast-throated, he follows her like

a tracking shot that took the crew three weeks to stage. With days
drenched in despondent night, they mutiny through stasis, resist

> CUT TO: *Again, that infernal clock.*
> *Train car hemorrhaging, roof*
> *top scaled. An ellipsis.*

the throttling of the hours toward shopping carts glutted with ailment.
These railways run parallel but incongruent; one stretches toward

longing, the other hunts for omission. They sleep in the wind of radio
static. She sways for the unthreaded fishhook. He is a desert gawking

> CUT TO: *Suitcase. Flower print dress.*
> *Unrequited knock at brass*
> *gates. Clock, grief-stricken.*

in Dutch tilt at the inebriated street that spurned him. Reviled Coke
bottles. Bedroom slippers under the vanity caught in soft focus.

Castigated like a dipsomaniacal gumshoe by the blunted edge
of minutes. Triangulated cravings asphyxiate them. Each tantalizes

CUT TO: *Pearl earring gifted to*
                 the second thief once
                 reclaimed from the first.

the other through taciturn tides of withholding. Hell-bent on boring
the sea. But this mise-en-scène does not belong to them. This

is the viewer's Malebolge, a whorl of truancy spliced from B-rolls
of rambunctious prodigals who refuse to catch what they chase.

CUT TO: *Clock. Stairwell in need*
                 of serenading. Threat posing
                 as flirtation. Opening credits.

(Fade in)

➤ Disco Ballistics

friday nights we prep for hot
skirmishes. take three to five
business days to primp and pick out
duds. shave. apply makeup. contact
all accomplices. hail our platoon.
then a cab. breach the checkpoint

      with a wink. order a round of shots
      during tactical strike assemblies. stake
      out our first kill of the evening. flanked
      by chaise lounges and black lights.
      the beat drops in syncopation
      with our first village

raid. clink our cosmos like mac clips.
chuck disco ball grenades into middle
schools. flirt bump and grind. spawn
mushroom clouds in unisex bathroom
stalls. flick cigarettes sucked
to the filter onto the casualties

      we create. the styles we pilfer. smack
      lips in the mirror. launch glitter drone
      assassinations. snipe the bartender's
      digits. swipe high-security specs
      detailing an after-party in Kabul. drop
      big tips like food rations into Yemen.

barrage insurgents with shock and awe
of strobe lights and unsanctioned
gropes. engage in a war of attrition
with the dj. execute a fashion victory
march through the city square. retreat
to a downtown studio loft bunker. order

a stop-loss for champagne brunch
in the meatpacking district. debrief
platoon on the briefs graves pearls
buried and plundered. court-martial
the sun for insubordinate conduct
during the ceremonial walk of shame.

⇒ Cicatristes (Demo Version)

who tucked you in   who tucked
you   brought you to the park
who tucked you brought you

lemonheads   baseball cards
marbles who tucked you
touched you   brought you

the dark you feared who touched you
when he tucked you   told you
it was supposed to make you

smile but you did could
would should   not smile
when he tucked you
brought you   whittled you

into alabaster who tucked you
in also taught you   alphabet
and shared his nerds with you

read to you stole you stickers
before he tucked you
read you fed you dark and now

you laugh because it cauterizes
the conundrum the humdrum
to recall who gave you the word

the sour stomach who tucked you
slit and gauzed you gave you
first aid and who granted you

the means   to read it

tiled floor bedecked
sepia of potato
chip wrappers wet
newspapers rusty nails
gym shoe musk
ambling through unkempt
hallways fissure fresco
of soda stains
ailing fidget spinners
computer lab windows
swathed in shroud
of dollar store
electrical tape incorrigible
asbestos cavities hum
cancer anthems dipped
in chocolate fluorescent
lights dial supplications
above bulletin board
molting pastel homilies
to auto repair
diorama sprawled across
webster avenue crowing

ANCIENT CIVILIZATIONS
UNIT STUDY
EGYPTIAN GODS
AND PHARAOHS

⟶ Human Instamatic

after Martin Wong

Roach motel in cinders.
Electromagnetic hand jive. Interregnum of Alphabet

City. Dilapidated voices from 1981
rescinded. Secret
Caribe Suzuki walk. Brick-hearted papi

chulos dressed   for anabasis. Handball
court liturgies. Little Ivan
of the Aztec jungle prays before
drowning in concrete.

Baked curbsides incite   the butcher to adorn
his quinceañera gown,
kiss a wireman
before sweaty tenements perfumed

in pitorro. Expired hydrants
mimic Cepheus, wait to be

rezoned. Boxed
in. Boxed up.
Boxed out.

Hopscotch dereliction among the scree.
Morir de angustia. Community
garden pig roast. Courtroom shocker.
He's got wrecking-ball lungs, hickory
smoked

ribs belting bachata for nine weeks
and counting. A pockmarked marquee
citing Ephesians.
Mystery sludge

crawls, congeals into a pond.
It's no place to raze, to raise

a raza, she raps.

Desespera siempre,
        negrito, siempre desaparecidos.

Gas mask revelation, paper lamps
bequeathed to repo lots.

Benevolent diss associations. Insolent departures
        from blue-faced angels
        named Angel who dawdle

in the basement with botanica candles.

Silence indicted, offered a plea deal. But the sitter
        is a despot vowing

                Cocotazos para todos!

What I saw was
what I meant was
what was was.

                Southbound, a roving vigil
                for the sundered. Northbound,

        an impaired fleet
        of unemployed demagogues
                        recolonizing the pool

hall. The Rubble Kings resurrected as testimonios
stricken from public record.

"Puerto Rico Is Burning Its Dead"

(Secuelas de María)

A lariat of subtractions, Aguadilla is enkindled,
Coamo is immolated. Twelve cadavers found,
but only one permitted burial. A wall of blank
epitaphs strangulates every province of flotsam.
The carrions of San Germán form a pyramid
of anthracite siphoned through loopholes
expunging each loss from the sum total.
Mayagüez has become a crematorium. Cut
off from their prescriptions, the seniors
are enlisted to clog the aqueducts with their
extremities. Puerto Rico is burning its dead.
The grief-stricken ashes are expelled data
offering contrition to the brass. Crippled
funeral parlors obliterate forensics, the sky
replete with muted quarter tones of lamenting
townsfolk destined to live as smoke. All accounts
of the aftermath have been redacted for the foreign
press. Those with bloodlines woven into the gardens
of San Lorenzo and Las Marías drown themselves
in unlit waiting rooms, unsure if hearing the names
of the vanished will ignite relief or calamity. There
is a burning if they make the list, a burning if they
continue to exist without punctuation. Their numbers
stifled by daft incumbents that refuse to comment.
Oxygen is put on the black market. Bones are used
to hold up infected roofs. Unidentified remains
get poured like concrete into jilted lungs. Dialysis
stations shuttered, the filing cabinets wielding
death certificates have dissolved into the Añasco.
Tonight Tres Picachos is nine feet closer
to the exosphere, hoisted by the monolith
of undocumented skulls accruing at its saddle.
The basin retooled into an oven to incinerate
the unmentionables. While smoldering, siblings
debate if it was hurricane or insouciance

that induced the disaster. The parched wounds
are left festering in Aguas Buenas and Yabucoa
as the head office determines what is a person
and what is collateral. Clouds cover bawling
electrical lines typecast as severed umbilical
cords. Puerto Rico is burning. Its dead, forever
exhumed, grieve over the phalanx of survivors.
They plead for definition. For cause. For first
responders. A single overheating generator
must keep the nation treading. Elihu Root's
brood goes viral. Caustic, they ask the departed,
Are you carcass or rumor? This pyre of a colony
left to singe the eyes of all witnesses from sierra
to shore. Converting kin into ether. A double
ghosting crowned by an auction. Cataclysm
spun as plum with financial prospects. Puerto
Rico is burning its dead. The subcontractors
have all walked off the job as the bereaved
keep counting. Keep foraging. Keep shipping
rations. Keep combing coast and summit
for every vanished tía. Keep mourning this
brownout with luster like aurora borealis.

Areyto for the Shipwrecked: Lost Articles

The

aliens

the
the

the

the   the

the

an

the

the

the

the

a

a

the

10.

Nineties kids called whatever we admired *the bomb.*

9.

When no one laughs at a comedian's jokes, we say he bombed.
If the comedian inspires peals of laughter, we say he killed
tonight, or she knocked them dead. The act of killing creates
regurgitation of noise, the slayed leave satisfied, while

the defining characteristic of bombing is callous silence. Is
the distinction a matter of timing, of rhythm? Is the dying
dependent on creating a conducive environment? Or is it
about complicity? When the crowd rejects the comedian's

joke there is fallout without detonation, the dissatisfaction
crushing the room's morale. If the joke solves Mark Twain's
equation of humor equals tragedy plus time, the laughter
will become pandemic, and the comic lays claim to the kill.

8.

Bombing in comedy is usually due to one
or more of the following factors: the word choice is stale,

the comic's timing and tone are asynchronous, their point
of view trite or overused. And Twain's equation is not duly

employed. Perhaps there was tragedy but the timing was off,
or tragedy was not employed with wit and grace. Some jokes

are *too soon,* others are insensitive to the audience's world-
view. It is possible that the comic misread the room, was *tone-*

deaf in their delivery. Without proper execution of these
elements the comic misfires and the joke does not land,

as they say in the business. It was a dud. The joke is unable
to light the fuse of the limbic system, thus no guffaw erupts.

If after discharging a joke only coughing and the clack of pint
glasses can be heard, the comic is marooned, left alone on

stage to wonder if this will be their last gig. It didn't land.
They bombed.

7.

In 1950, American jet fighters struck the towns of Jayuya
and Utuado. It was one of two occasions in which the U.S.
bombed its own citizens. Some Puerto Ricans had made it

clear that they were not thrilled about being occupied by
organizing a rebellion to expel the invaders. In response
to this insurrection, the foreign sovereign bombed civilians.

If one were to make the analogy that the foreign sovereign
is to the island as the comic is to the club, then the imposed
citizenship is a joke that did not land and the rebellion is equal

to heckling the comic. The hack foreign sovereign hated being
heckled, could not tolerate having bombed, so they opened fire.
The bombing of the cities was a surprise. Surprise has long

been a trusted tool of the comic. It can be applied by exploiting
the ambiguity of a phrase or by abruptly shifting a story's
focus. The trick is to challenge your audience's expectations.

Here, no one expected they would bomb civilians. This one
landed. The hecklers were silenced. It was tragedy. Plus time.
Whereas with comedy both comic and crowd are pleased when

the joke lands, this form of bombing leaves only the bomber
sated. Leaves only the bomber. The bomb lands. The crowd
demands their money back. But there will be no refund.

6.

On Fordham Road, two Kings are busted for bombing

the Family Welcome Center. Their black and purple

throwie reads *Life B 4 Cash*. The court will frame them

as felons, but the graffing is just them biting off

the forefathers, the original tag-bangers who

slammed the Six Grandfathers—hallowed terrain

of the Lakota, the Cheyenne, the Arapaho, the Kiowa—

with a colossal burner of granite and mica schist

plugging Washington, Jefferson, Roosevelt, Lincoln.

5.

The former bomb is a joke that didn't land, landing
the kids on probation. The latter bomb is a desecration
of land, a silence bolstered by shrapnel of tourism.
The bomb was seen as a joke to some, though it isn't

4.

exactly funny.

3.

Graffers bomb to exert their right to create, to reclaim
grifted territory. If you say you bombed the J train, your
claim has two concurrent meanings. First, it means you
branded the train, and thus the landscape, with your
personal style, so the train belongs to you, at least
until the city cleans the train or another writer bombs
your piece. Second, it means that you have beautified
a space that was intentionally made ugly by private
interests. So, you see, bombing is both an act of sedition
and of addition. When graffiti writers bomb the surface
of a thing, they are planting orchids in an ash heap.

2.

An antipode to when Trump bombed Syria,
or when Obama bombed Yemen, or when Clinton
        bombed Kosovo, or when Bush bombed
        Iraq, or when Reagan bombed Beirut,
or when Nixon bombed Cambodia,

or when Eisenhower bombed Korea, or when
        Truman bombed Japan. Those bombings
        did not beautify, resurrect, or give birth,
though the bombers were aiming to lay claim
over a territory in an inversion of what graffers

                        call *going all-city.*

1.

Whenever comics bomb, the silence
it engenders is followed by yawning.

Whenever graffiti writers bomb,
the silence it engenders is followed

by awe or a summons. Whenever
fighter planes bomb, the

    0.

–1.

*(Multivalent in its application, the single common characteristic of bombing
is that in all scenarios the act is perceived to be an endpoint in, or interruption
to, a charted course, a proposed solution to a lack: of imagination, of resources,
of joy. Both the bomber and the bombed are now inextricably coupled. Both
permanently altered.)*

ACT TWO

"Between shark and gull how . . ."

Édouard Glissant

⇒ Fox & Foghorn

after Tim Seibles

Beware of bunnies
dressed in drag! Beware of samurai-
sword-wielding terrapins! Watch for anvils
descending from above like secret
telegrams! Here rodents
in diapers pirouette through pantries
teasing felines permutated
into accordions played by hungry
mutts in moonlit piazzas! Beware
of chattering teakettles
and precocious swine slinging
oranges and old leather shoes! Here
nothing is as deadly as a subversive
ironing board blasted
like a bazooka into rubber-
band torsos! Watch for the ricochet
of flying fruit! Steer clear of ACME
merchandise fated to fall
apart faster than a celebrity
marriage! Here we are raised
cell by cell by smarmy
hens determined to deceive us
with mountains disguised as open
highways meant to flatten
faces reinflated with a bicycle
pump stashed in overalls! Beware
of blueberry pies baked
with TNT served to singing
ducks in top hats! Do not take
offense to being blown to bits
by exploding cigars,
for in the next frame we return
to the scene spotless and chasing
a sarcastic woodpecker
wearing a gorilla suit

into a rabbit hole! Never eat ham
sandwiches made by pistol-toting
horses! Whenever bearded
feet shove a shotgun in your eye
do not hesitate to tie the barrels
into a pretty bow! Here hazards
come in adorable packages!
Furniture has a social life! Fish
sing in three-part harmony!
Their watercolor habitat
hilarious, two-dimensional and sentient!
Here the supreme
survival tool is a boundless
fondness for the senseless!

⟶ Cicatristes (Acoustic Version)

Called you brother when he needed an accomplice,
      when he soiled himself and buried his boxers
behind the garage. Asked you to be lookout. You,
      too young to understand what you were supposed
to be looking for. Called you nephew at school,
      compelling a coterie of classmates to follow you
home and force-feed you gravel, their odium
      an inheritance from their older brothers whose
execrations contaminated the room you shared.
      Called you cousin after learning his mother
was really his sister, genealogy reshuffled fifteen
      years after his birth. Called you with blighted hush
while tickling you in the dark too long, too late,
      too close to your secret grotto, his phalanges
acting as interlopers until you grew to walk sideways,
      unsure of all the ways the fondling impaired you.
Called you man when you weren't, coercing two
      older girls to cosset you on Northern Boulevard
against grates, unripe pears and the residue of Mike
      and Ikes grafted to the back of your teeth. Calls
out to you now on holidays neither of you celebrate
      to ask about your wife and inquire why you never
write back. The family calls your inanition cold,
      spoiled. They file you under arrogant for sculpting
yourself into a reticent plinth. You call the aphasia

      an heirloom.

Reciprocal Aubade for My Scopophiliac

What thorny impotence has steeped you
into this kink? So this is how you want me—

veiled, stripped? For what boils you is leering
at an exposed sliver of waist, a birthmark

that protrudes from a naked heel. Your cool
fetish is to slip me your card and your keys,

promising me I can take what I want, go
where I please, while you bug my bodice.

Is this what inflames your collar? Perching
the circuitry of your mineral eye across

the street from my place of work? Leaving
recipes in my sock drawer? Does it stiffen

your iris to gaze at me shedding the puce
dress you gave me on our anniversary,

poking your head out from behind the face
of a week-old newspaper? I would offer you

the chance to taste my tunic, to weigh me
on the marble slab of your lap, but I'm afraid

for you contact is as thrilling as a wart. You
covet not to pet me but to collect another

pet, to have my aroma pulled over you
without having to accede to the oil of touch.

A ribald murmuration, you demand for my
no to mean yes, use the words *probe*

and *investigate* as lurid dalliance, a skein
of surveillance tapes uncoiling, lavender-

scented creams applied to cloaked domains.
You pretend to be absent when I wipe

the soil from my neck, tell me this is the last
time, it's over, until tomorrow night when

you return to peek from behind the bushes
in my front yard. I will leave the bedroom

window ajar, because paranoia is our
foreplay, the tight clamp of your taloned

pupil peeping through a bramble of firewalls
keeps us both panting. And I'll complain

that you give me no space, but we both know
it would dismantle me if you ceased to feel me

up with wiretaps and seize my server because
you are certain I'll find you milksop and stray.

Will it tingle you when you learn my password
is our safe word? If you ever came to corner

me, to blow in my ear, would you even know
how to unwrap me? Would you be sated?

Darling Devourer, trust the febrile kisses I pin
to my site are for you and you alone. Now

start the tape. Hold yourself, pulsing and stout.
If you promise not to finish too soon, I promise

to share with you every curve and crater
of my most lambent moon as it abates.

Latinxorcismos: Semiotic Study of the Gringo Horror Film (Required Reading)

The killer is always Brown. Even when they aren't. The killer
is Brown and not human. A damp alien drenched in scales.
Shell-backed, their wrecked ship mangles the corn field.
Or they're ghost. An intruder who has always been here
hovering. Ghostly and transparent but nevertheless Brown.
An autochthonous stranger clawing at the wainscoting,
sprouting from sacred ground. You can count on mention
of sacred ground. Defiled. The rational plea of a burnt specter
mistaken for houndwail because the family of the house live
monolingually. The house itself installed over an unmarked
grave. The Brown howling from the basement, a plea. A howl
that preceded the basement. Or the town itself. Though
no one seems to recall this ginger wraith with many
tongues ever living there. Now they whisper rust-flavored
secrets through the floorboards, announce their refusal
to leave. Reciting the secret unleashes fire, so the viewer
is taught to tread lightly through the halls and cover their
own mouth, to never speak the Name, an admission of all
they've shuttered up in the walls, a secret about the family
and how they acquired the house, the woman

> they buried to possess it. She is a mist in a hollow. Always
> hollow. A mist who does not carry the mortgage but insists
> on haunting the gang from the suburbs who just camped
> here for fun, moved in to flee some addiction, bought
> the place because it was cheap and came with a caretaker
> who is also Brown. Brown and loyal, but not to be trusted,
> says a green sheriff with a drawl. The sheriff also warns
> nice visitors to keep an eye out for Strangers. Strangers
> are frowned upon in these parts. When he says Strangers
> he means Brown. See, all these new residents really want
> is a quiet spot to raise children or fix their marriage,
> and Brown only comes to disturb it, bursting through
> the walls as blood-drenched omen. This used to be a nice
> place, the green sheriff says, before the auburn swarm

arrived, returned, refused to leave or whatever,
and now none of the light bulbs work and every day
is a fog of sharpened incisors, and the citizens have
all gone sick from digging up tombs where their pools
should be. All because some comemierda wraiths won't
stay dead, won't be banished, won't turn down their
music and accept subpar working conditions. Can't
even fish in the creek anymore without being dragged
to the bottom by a belligerent relic. Faith in the good
book just isn't enough to cast these phantoms back
into the nether regions built by CoreCivic for just
this purpose. This is going to take a rifle, some
gasoline, a couple of flares, and a booby trap nailed
to the old tractor. Once their arms are caught
in its claws and the remaining townsfolk douse
them in conviction, a blind old white woman
is dragged into the frame to perform an utterance,

one that will drive the tawny spirits out of the cellar
and back into the cupboard to fix supper for the master
of the house that is also their sepulchre. And there
are children, always children screaming for help, aimed
to garner sympathy so the new inhabitants are not
blamed when they dump the ashes of the enemy onto
the steps of the courthouse, because they've already
got the neighbors believing Brown is succubus, djinn
and imp risen from beneath, and the pestilent coop
they've pitched around what's left of amber specters
is entirely for the viewer's protection. As credits
empty the seats, the threat is shown one last time
to announce there will be a sequel, cast in silhouette,
or just their boots, a close-up of their gloved hands
clenched around the steering wheel where
they have taken their place as the relentless,
                    resentful chauffeur for the white protagonist
                    who, above all else, fears requital, redress.

⇒ *Sleep Dealer* (dir. Alex Rivera, 2008)

Dry, this mesa. What is potable siphoned
by droneshepherds warding these hinter-
lands. Their lenses sniff me hyperpoaching
company waves. Delete my source code,
spurring migration via system integration.
My rural gone obsolete. Bail to cop work

as dermal conduit. Repurposed by coyotech. Ahora soy
prosthetic stoop labor. Discarnate appendages uprooting

cassava via livestream. The innovation
this demesne of capital gain has sought:
an interface that unBrowns the goods.
Each hour spent betahitched to network
of cybermaquilas surges my amaurosis.
Neural bandwidth atrophies when chains

go asomatous. Mi memoria outsourced to depleted
sectors, embezzled and greased to snooze pilferers.

Nodehunted. Ramsacked. My narco-
processors watt-sapped, until Luz hemo-
hacks wetware syncretism. Until meta-
carpal of droneshepherds hits ctrl-alt-
del. Hops mode and margin. Excises
ill logic gate that robohews granjero

from extranjero. Inducing BitTorrent deluge of ancient
rain to el campo. Leveejack. Bolt for new motherboard.

Illegal my eyes.　　　　Iris of unfertilized
plateaus.　　　Unforgiven　　for surging
into a dialect　　with no global market
value. Illegal my argot.　　　　　　　I cannot
just wade out　　in neutral lakes. I cannot
say.　　Cannot evade the plexus that marks
me contraband.　　　　　When I seed above
ores you crave you illegal me, forge deeds,
uproot me,　　　hire me to manage the waste,
illegal my soles　　　　when your arsons　　　drag
me to your doorstep. Illegal my faith.
Broadcast me　　an illegal substance.　　Refuse
me lodging　　if I refuse to be free　　labor.
Allege me vermin,　　　toxin,　　zombify all
kin who return　　　enraged by your tombopolis.
Illegal my relics, confiscate my liver.　　Now
even my scars　　must be registered.　　Illegal
my pyres　　enkindled by your　　rote
pandemics.　　Illegal the bronze of my cutis.
If I split walnuts　　　with the neighbors
somehow it's lascivious.　　　Illegal my
parchments,　　my pons,　　my corybantic
time signatures.　　　　Only my silence
is welcome. Only my silence　　is suspect.

On Appropriation

      The time I said it, it was me, Big T, Sammy, Jay Dee,
and Mills. We were owning the bleachers at our school
basketball game, ignoring the score, the raucous boilerplate
pageant of male bravado was a flu caught from our fathers'
garages and sports highlight reels. Dishing out digs about
mothers, flicking earlobes, a carom of elbows eking to topple
whoever stood on the loftiest tier. Mills cut at my hair, calling
it a *halfro*, launching Skittles at the back of my head to see

if they'd bounce or get lost in my poorly gelled drey,
his disses encroaching the line between the jesting
of middle school boys and a formal act of treason. Chafing
from these slams, I cracked back, snapping *Oh, this* ▮▮▮▮▮
thinks he's funny. The word hung like a fermata for three
measures too long, the caesura broken by the crowd
huffing about a bad call down on the court. One by one
their retinas revoked me, imparting me with an axiom

I should have known: though none of our forebears slept
in the big house, their bisabuelos were chained to trapiches,
while my bisabuelo was most likely ordained to wield the lash
that struck them. Sammy and Jay Dee, their skin tattooed
with the hard *R* of their dialect, quickly affixed themselves
to the game as if to expunge my infraction. Mills fashioned his
lats into a moat dividing us, his fist scorched from clenching.
I leaned toward Big T, my oldest friend, who once teased me

that the peach fuzz on my lip was a turnpike billboard that
begged *deport me*, who joked that every roach was my cousin,
who I had shared bunks and vacationed with, whose mother
dressed my wounds when I fell in the park. Big T, who had
been given an all-access pass to our refrigerator by my own
mother. I looked to him for backup, and he, too, stranded
me with the casta carcass I had carelessly dragged out
into our town square, a frigid reminder that being spawned

from the same archipelago did not mean I could claim
ownership of their blackness, for I would never be placed
into a lower track at school before even being tested. My tint
had never provoked purse clutching. Stop and frisk was not
scripted to wrangle me. I never had to worry that a police
officer might empty a chamber into my spine knowing
his job was not at stake. I was their friend, and they might
protect me from bullies, they might share their bat and ball

and answers to the test with me, but that word was not mine
to wield. I had no right to speak it or to ask them to offer
me license to use it, even though my memory told me I had
rapped Snoop and Ice-T lines with them and never skipped
those two syllables. But maybe I did. Two class periods later,
Big T handed me his headphones so I could hear the new Tribe
track. The next day Sammy met me, as always, at the 86th Street
courts for our weekly one-on-one. As if I had never jeopardized

the Alliance. Within a week, Mills dropped by to whoop me
in Sega baseball. And I was still invited to horror movie night
at Jay Dee's for Halloween. They all offered me mercy, never
once mentioned my violation. Big T, Sammy, Jay Dee, and Mills,
they forgave me for confusing blood with skin, taught me that
it wasn't merely a matter of hue that I could not say it. It is also
because those who hold up their whiteness like a coat of arms
pleasure themselves by uttering the word. They blister with

the temptation to fill their jaws with it. It stokes their sadist
hearts to yelp it and play the beasts they fear they never were.
Grateful for the amnesty my crew bestowed me, I swore I would
not recklessly unsheathe those syllables again, for love may
prove to be unconditional, but it does not pardon those of us
who trample over provinces for which we hold no title.

"Give Me My Flowers While I Yet Live"

Hanged him in the family shed.

The family shed tears the color of elderberries.

The elders buried him in a grotto where the egg
factory dumped defective shells.

Detectives held a press conference claiming
that it was suicide and not a murder.

A murder of deputized crows defected
from their abandoned precincts to plant
false evidence for the guilty party.

The guilty partied in a loft looming over
the corroded edge of town, mixing
cocktails of crushed cadavers and home-
made bitters. It was a calculation
of stale corridors and court dates
wrought with counter-motions
and obfuscations littered throughout.

Litter obfuscated the thoroughfare
between the hanged man and his
legacy of conundrums.

This legacy of cons drummed up
feelings of lassitude and rueful
longing for a longer rope, or limbs

more limber than those his gods gave him.

Those gods gave him gout and a century
playing the alibi for his executioner.
But they promised the grotto
that now buttressed his lobes

would blossom into a planetarium,
an aviary, and an archive indicting
those that hanged him in the family shed.

("Yes, it happened.")

Nonstop from Fruitvale to Ursa Major: Ofrenda for Los Desaparecidos of the United States

for Oscar Grant, et al.

A lung lit like diesel
is not fable or fodder.

Is not sewage siphoned from stern
and starboard.   Cuffs, not slapdash plums,
plunge from your garden. A labor
of moles audit your liver.
         Unquenchable tasers huddle around
you like a gaggle of bleak midwives.

         A diesel-lit lung is not a gift
from the mayor,
         for a name is not a plaque,
is not an anthem composed to arouse
         a hemoglobin-parched stadium.

Self-taunted, they label you Anger
         as they flit with anger.
         Their fear scantily
clad, colluding in a prim commune armed
with hedge clippers.
         Grandiloquently, they rattle

inside haughty cages,
         send nescient sentinels to slip
         into ventricles,
siphoning mortgages and fractured treaties,
         terrified that you will offer tithes
         to the Patron Saint of Reciprocity.

Argent,   you are the new nebula,
         a rucksack of pitted olives,
         an escrache
         sullying the real

                    estate cult of rubber
                    bullets and dank paddy wagons.

Your lung lit like diesel
bursts,   spirals upward,
                        pulling unstoppable
            phosphors into its orbit.

ACT THREE

" . . . for this salt, this oil."

Etel Adnan

Once Upon a Time in Anatolia
(dir. Nuri Bilge Ceylan, 2011)

Our narrator is an exhausted desert
mumbling through a scuzzy window.

Establishing shot: a kilim
of silk hillsides where the men
are built with basalt and the women exist only as vapor.

A squall wheezes woe into bent shovels and laptops. A motorcade

of wounded cigarettes stalks
this balloon-lit corpse
that the centuries refuse to inter. The suspect
and the medical examiner

are fields of hüzün shot in rack focus.
The prosecutor is a pasha
of slog and revel.
He is fulcrum for the bickering
bureaucrats shaking the peninsula
like a tree whose dates

have evicted themselves from an ambivalent parable. This caravan

tarries and fidgets,
devout as a fable.
They await the magic hour to carry
out the postmortem.

But the suspect is a lamp
consumed by moths
and cannot seem
to remember where
he left his anti-miracle.

Once swathed in a frisson of buffalo yogurt and lamenting
hypothetical bir tanem who portend their own autopsy,

                                    the battalion slow zooms
                        wayward into a guilt-
                              infused blackout.

Their work trousers sequestered from the scorn of headlights,
              each is unsure about whether
                        they are the knife,
        the butcher, or the lamb.

                              The dilated fields lead
                              them into an exquisite hovel
                              beneath Mount Erciyes

where the mayor's daughter emerges from the kitchen
as a halo of ginger tea and penance.

              Shaken by their own leers, they confess

                        to the decadence of soiled lungs. Dawn
                        invites them to uproot
                        the cadaver they fed

        to the trunk. The commissar relinquishes
                              a cigarette to the suspect. A soccer ball

is retrieved and returned to the stream
that bisects inconsolable empires.

⇒ Cicatristes (Extended Club Version)

this uncle. now your cousin. respired with. tenebrous lungs.
now told. to call him. Brother. vernal. spooked by. abuelo's
whip. cracked when ham. and eggs. go uneaten. begs to be

forgiven by. the belt. like a night-light. spotlights contusions.
highlights doors left ajar. in his forehead. no campfire could
keep. wasps away from. sugar sullen mattress. whose bed-

springs. drilled him. that people come. shadowed in extra.
terrestrial. skin. BrotherUncleCousin miss. took him for. as.
mother won't for. give him. for telling. would not believe.

relieve him. receive him as. because mother was. sister.
while sister was. aunt. who raised him as. son until she
ran with. under her arm. leaving BrotherNephewSon with.

step. grand. parents. who confused him for. nothing. in
chastised light. you learned. to distrust the day. that hid.
everything in full view. yet blaze optics. so that no. one

may look directly. into one. an other. not BrotherUncle-
Cousin. or MotherSister. coddling an invalid daughter.
who birthed three. of her own. leaving them to Mother-

Sister. to mother them. as MotherGrandmother. mean-
while. the bodies. the den. lean into their own. ears
and whisper *why?* to heirs. of this mutual malaise. with

two eyes. no mouth. you chased away. with dark glasses.
an anamnesis. disown them. all. recrudescent patriarchy.
anaphylactic. in disrepair. but you. were soon adopted by

the night. the plague. inseminated. by the apocrypha.
and you. with a weaponized insomnia. to incinerate
denial. extricate the disenchanted. the quarantined

who surrender. to smashed dishes. maledictions. wage
vowels. to resurrect. the disemboweled. the discarded.
lure the blue with comets. cornets. break the legacy.

with breakbeats. blaring from rooftops. offering blood
to the anemic. to live as anathema. keep your pact
with the sleepless. to quiet the dysphoria. with a most

effulgent darkness. to endure the dimness of dawn.
so you might. witness the day. the depraved. sun.
                                would not rise. and return.

➤ **Core Curriculum Standards: Parkland, Belmont, Marshall County, Aztec, Rancho Tehama, Townville, Marysville, Reynolds, Arapahoe, Sparks, Sandy Hook, Chardon, Nickel Mines, Platte Canyon, Red Lake, Rocori, Red Lion, Santana, Columbine, et al.**

Paroxysm. Shrapnel cafeteria emits epiphanies in pond ripples.
Editorials of shredded children summoning psychics to deliver
them crib sheets cryo-frozen as sound bites. Film seduces grievers
to sign waivers. Websites worship the click click. Baited. Debased.
By demagogues pregnant with conquistador's lymphoma. Discharge.
Hollow-point. Castrate. From Big Bang. To Columbine. To Newtown.
To Fort Hood. To Charleston. To Pulse. To Mandalay Bay. Phantom
forked tongue recoils open veins echoed in rifle shell blowback.
Blown away like minds in altered states. Catatonic state served
by superdelegates while the blame is placed on rap stars manacled
to 360 deals. Screens project smoke rising from barrels into seer
suited petroglyphs. Guitar riff. Monolith of liquidated carcasses
refinanced. Blood cells consummate with bludgeoned milk cartons.
Two intersecting rivers. Slipping like arrow from quiver. To neutralize
rebellious chiefs defending the tribe from assimilation. Bodies slump
to earth like an ice-cream cone on concrete. Panic lab concoction.
Gore labyrinth diverting survivors to a landfill of martyrs. Market
research determines all four demographic quadrants think murder
be optimal method of ousting sour musk of revisionist history. Red
eye cured with white lie. With textbooks drenched in rote timeline
of war dates. Aguirre's descendants reproduce excavation with .40
caliber peacocking. Drunk on atomic promise. Rigor mortis rigmaroles.
Cult of masculinity passed off as divine purpose. Militias sprouting
like galleons traveling westward. Plague and swarm. Bullet hole
becomes black hole. Entropy envelops a schoolteacher hiding
her kids in the closet. As barrels aim skyward. Hollow-tipped.
To make effigies of shadows. Of daughters permanently suffused
to walls at Nagasaki. Some call it collateral consequence. Call hatchet
men terrorist when burnt umber. Call it mental health issues. When
lynchmen are. Melanin-deficient. The virus, a void. Consumes itself
for more airtime. The muscle, a trigger. Triggers a muscle. A clause
in the contract. A blankness bequeathed by the estate. The legacy.
An illness of emptiness. Shapeless color. Matter without space.

Palatial parasite. Sterilized. Stellated imbroglio of pathogens.
Silencer pressed at hollow skull. Manufactured escorts to Coaybay.
A rerun of the virus. Of Wounded Knee. Of Ciénaga. Of Mozambique.
Of Ponce. Of Dos Erres. Of Tlatelolco. Of Sétif. Of My Lai. Of El Mozote.
Of Black July. Of Sand Creek. Of Matewan. Of Wilmington. Horizon line
subjugated. Extinguishing song and wilderness. Laughter muzzled.
By poltroon's surrogate instrument. Prelude to walkout. Paroxysm.

The Unscathed

gather in silos of saltshakers and folded
linen. They wait impatiently for another round

of green pills and butter pats, as if there were
no such thing as a precipice. In a few minutes

the factory will receive a rush order for more
artificial limbs, carafes filled with antidotes

are served to the unafflicted. The Unscathed
take leave of their plans to inhabit Montauk

for the month of August. Robust delivery
trucks obstruct the view of plasma drying

out on the boulevard. The Unscathed wonder
if it is too late to catch the Metro-North back

to the musicals they attended in the last
century. The bistro's grade is pending,

and starlings collude upon the bell tower,
waiting for the Unscathed to drop their pastry

crusts off at the nursery. Teapot. Meat grinder.
Cyanide kiss. A vale of eloquent vultures. School

will let out early this afternoon. The Unscathed
will receive a message reminding them that

blood is not thicker than pixels. Undulation.
Sigh. In just a few moments someone

at the bar will complain that they have
waited far too long for their check.

→ On Money

I wish more poets would write about money.
—Susan Briante, *The Market Wonders*

A man wipes clean his Salvatore Ferragamos before confessing to his tablemate that he's absolutely broke. So broke that he had to trade in his Cooper and cancel the yearly trip to Antigua.

/

Murat is fifteen years old. He sweeps the floors, polishes doorknobs, and for fifty cents he'll fetch your groceries for you. Murat cannot read, has never been to school. His father tells me, *If he's in school, we don't eat.*

/

A man craves a latte. He reaches into his wallet for a metaphor, one that will quell his thirst. He wants a new suit, so he flashes a plastic card with his name on it. His name is assigned a number that is branded on the card. The card is linked to an invisible cloud of numbers that swirl through a celestial database like a swarm of wasps, or a swarm of nano quadrotors, or like antigens through a bloodstream. The amount of metaphors embedded in his part of the cloud diminishes with each latte. The cloud multiplies like amoebas, then merges with larger clouds of skewed and disinterested data. The heat from the latte burns the man's tongue.

/

Before we conjured up money, we traded a thing for a thing, hauling our corn to the next farm in search of goat's meat. Corn husks are stripped and strewn about. Goat's flesh is butchered and cured. Blood seeps into the woodwork, leaving us responsible for the stains we create. Now money leaves us exchanging a thing for a promise, a vague impression that perfumes our vanity and our guilt. We offer religious tokens to the butcher, silver acts of faith, so our hands and our floors remain unblemished. We promise the butcher our offering will ensure his own son the opportunity to eat without branding his hands with blood.

/

Wu-Tang Clan yell *Cash rules everything around me*. Aloe Blacc pleads *I need a dollar dollar dollar, that's what I need*. M.I.A. proclaims *All I wanna do is pow pow pow pow ka-ching ching and take your money*. Audio Bullys promise *If I had a hundred million I would probably give half to you*. The Dead Kennedys scream *Kill kill kill kill kill the poor!* Motörhead direct you to *Eat the rich*. Pink Floyd threaten *Keep your hands off my stack*. The Beatles whine *You never give me your money*. N.A.S.A. chimes the cliché that *Money money money money money is the root of all evil*. All of them a choir singing in affirmation, or condemnation, or combing for converts.

/

Pizarro, before stretching his boots toward the peaks of Peru, stretched his battered paw out toward investors who would underwrite his descent into the unknown. Their contract was a litany, devout faith that he would return to them with profit. Pizarro and his backers spouted conversion as their mission. The act of religious conversion was a means to convert Latin America's wealth into Europe's wealth. Faith in god was faith in gold, committed by excising the Inca's faith in Atahualpa. When Pizarro erected the name of their European god before the Western Hemisphere, it was a utilitarian act, not a blind trust in canonical scripture, for the collective faith of their investors is what endowed them with the power to seize what was not theirs.

/

. . . And when Adam Smith professed his unconditional belief in the "Invisible Hand of the Market," was it not an act of devout religious faith?

/

The choir echoes through the ATM chapels.
Tithes are collected.

Our sins are forgiven,
or at least stricken from the record.
We inch closer to our very own
townhouse in heaven.

/

Money has become the weather,   a collection of unruly
environmental conditions   pushing   across   the
ethosphere.   Three billion dollars   dart
across the sky between sunrise and sunset,   bouncing from
satellite to bank to bar to car rental to telephone to hotel to newsstand—
        an uncontrollable march of imperceptible sums approaching like a
tsunami.   Its patterns of movement are obsessively
researched and predicted   like a meteorologist working
to prophesize the possibility of rain tomorrow.   This
migration of symbols, of artificial signifiers, instantly materializes
        and disappears   from one spatiotemporal
location   to another   causing
droughts,   floods,   fallouts,
        sandstorms,

                and, on rare occasions,
                                sunshine.

/

        My wife and I drive past
the Hustler club and she shocks me
by saying she feels pity for the men inside.
        I ask her, what about the women?

Well, the women too, of course, she says,
        *but that one is obvious. The men
are a murkier brand of sad. The women
are there because this climate*

offers few options for work. But the men
are there because they do not know how
           to talk to women. They have no
clue how to connect. These men lack charm.

They simply are not sensitive enough
in speech and act to make a woman feel
close enough to want to disrobe for them.
           So they rely on money to be their wit,

           their surrogate for authentic
seduction. For them money is the pill
for this deficiency of allure, a placebo
for grace, the language of the lonely.

           /

Mom says it's rude to ask someone how much they make.

     ///

➤ Insolvency

Callow.   I once wore you like a limp.
You were throttling and you clung to my waist.
I crowded around the fire exit to the theater

hoping flecks of star carrion might flake off
and pollinate my mouth, and I would find myself
no longer mortified by the persistence of hunger.

Certain there was more than one way
to stop the water from rising,
                I hunted down keys for the canal locks.

My ear canals singed,   I coveted guaníns
I had no part in shaping. I devoured lampposts
and out-of-tune bicycle racks.   Maimed.

I limped in honor of your cellophane blush
and the rats roosted
                in asphalt that threatened

to unveil me and denounce the rehearsed crimp
in my posture.   I was frigid
beneath sycamore sewer lines where we last

        pretended to be thunder.
I wanted the floor to rise
                without having to pay

the debt in bouts of nausea. I wanted to not need
the weight of compliments and I wanted to be
the melody that warded off

                        the catcalls of accountants
and traffic wardens.   Wingless.   I caroused
through convention halls hocking sofa covers

and commemorative plates.   Defaulted.
I slipped on the epoxy of the ballroom floor
                              and into a moss of parrhesia.

Areyto for the Shipwrecked: Re/Vuelta

                                        The agaves, the passion
fruit that enveloped me, the silver earmarked for markets beyond

these tropics, they compel you to post outfits at the foot of my bed.
Each morning you blitzkrieg the tavern and pineapple conucos,

turn the rivers into arsenic, lock my kin up in sheet metal factories,
committing autopsies on their bodies while they are still alive.

You ask me to leave. You ask me to return, mounting electrified
fences around my springs and mineral deposits. You bottle up

the reservoir of my birth and ask me to pay, but I have no currency.
You cut the Aymara, the Quechua, the Lokono from my uvula, pry

me from the vines that nursed me, relocate me to a fiberglass
asylum. Tell me to leave my farm fallow. Indict me when I protest,

when I beg to be buried next to my mother. You ask me to leave.
You ask me to return. You irrigate my daughter's veins, widow

me with your excavations, post eviction notices on my hearth
and render me a vagrant in my own roost. When I scale

the Andes to nest in the backyard of your vacation home,
you drop the red flag and cry encroachment. With a single

papaya, I then camp beneath a bridge, lay a blanket across
your metropolis of dismembered mainframes. You send

subpoenas, coin me trespasser. You ask me to return, you ask
me to leave, demand I make myself useful if I am to stay. I repair

your appliances, put up drywall, pick your apples, polish your
porcelain, raise your kids who never see you because you are in

my country putting up luxury townhouses, carving my cousins
into chattel. From your detritus I harvest a new family, subsisting

on only prayer and memory. Feed my kids tomes you abandon
in landfills until the youngest siphons the venom from your syntax,

miracles your numerals, and earns a seat in the academy
next to your offspring. Now you demand a refund on what

you stole. You stifle me after I unearth your cooked books,
smear me for dismantling the guillotine circus you pitch

on my stoop, then dispatch an assistant to offer a settlement
of rotten tripe. When I show you a deed to the land, you

mispronounce my name. You create a shortage of spikenard.
Invent the idea of *North*. You hock haute couture coups.

Make a lullaby of my wounds. Then you ask me to leave.
You ask me to return. To return. To leave. To return. To. To

Mutiny at the Elder Care Facility

Had to summon four orderlies and my aunt
to confiscate the knife bisabuela stashed in
her bloomers. She held the pilfered blade
to her chest like a cross as the impious
attempted to strip this shiv that was her
only protection. From what? At ninety,
bisabuela drives the men of the home
to act like hormone-glutted teens. They
pitch their wheelchairs before her wing
in hopes of catching one whiff of her
Vicks VapoRub. She got all Roberto
Durán on one for trying to woo her
during *Sábado Gigante*. These last six
weeks no nurse's aide has been able
to wash or feed her. She doesn't need
them. Anyone. When viper-headed ex-
husbands deracinated her plot of ginger
she swayed like a weary banyan but
never cracked. And when despots
occupied the coasts and forced her
to replant herself in a city that worked
double shifts to give her hypothermia,
she was a bulwark. She staged her own
brand of insurgency by turning deaf
to their language, vowing to one day
reclaim her villita and never set foot
on this godforsaken continent for all
her remaining days. But her damn kids.
They did make her return. For what?
Just because she left the stove on one
time? Now some infant in scrubs insists
on wiping her. Well she's had enough.
Coño. She's keeping the knife. Whoever
thinks about taking it, or anything else
from her, can be sure to feel its bite.

Anthropomorphic Study of the Antilles

Parabola of mangroves in an equatorial yawn,
　　　blue dunes deflecting the Gaze that leers
　　　　　　at her glades and sierras. She dodges
　　　　　　　　　　lustful overtures to her
　　　　　　　　sun-drenched alcoves,
　　　　　　　　summons Guabancex to halt the erection
　　　　　　　　　　　　　of bitcoin brothels fencing her

　　basins and charging membership fees. When
　　　　　　　　　she insists that she is not
　　　　　　property, cannot be consumed
　　　　　　　　　for private pleasure, the Gaze collects
　　　　　　　　　armies and lawyers, draws up

　　　　　　　　　　charters that she is forbidden
　　　　　　to vote on. Her barrier reefs break
　　　　　　the tide of offenders lunging at her piers,
　　　　　　　　　scattering a season of pathogens

　　　　　　claiming her lots vacant as they stoop
　　　　　　　　　to appraise her star apples.
　　　　　　　　　　　Cornered, she stings,
　　　　　　　　　　　wades out into uncharted shoals

　　　　　　　　　　beyond earshot of chancellors
　　　　　branding her bruja and harlot, epithets she
　　　　　　mulls and ferments into a caney

　　　　　　　　　for her son Bayamanaco,
　　　　　　who burns the leeches listed
　　　　　　in the Panama Papers. She starves

　　　　　　　　　　　　them until they divest
　　　　and peel off their cara palos. They beg to lasso

her and teethe on her coral. She shakes

them loose, rattling her Beata Ridge

to make it plain she is not kept. They call her Sycorax,

but she is no foil in some sallow man's tale.

She is not grief-tinted or deprived,
no mere harbor

for the wanton and the loused, was not

put here for an Other's private

swashbuckling. Unbound

by syllogism, circumstellar
and circumspect, she adorns red

clay, is Milwaukee Deep,
gets all Kick 'Em Jenny on armadas
that approach without consent.

ACT FOUR

" . . . and a flag of hunger."

Hugo Margenat

My Commonwealth

after Ryuichi Tamura's "My Imperialism"

A lone mamey
blooms from the tower
of flaming wheels.

My Commonwealth reaches
to pluck it. My Commonwealth
starves beneath apocryphal winters.

*

I've got a dime, but no telephone.
While my Commonwealth is a satellite tumbling into the Pacific.

*

The teacher introduced my Commonwealth to the class
by saying that she was new to the school, but she has been
here since before there was such a thing as schools.
The teacher told the class to speak slowly to my
Commonwealth because she didn't know their
language, but my Commonwealth understood
everything they said. When students threw wads of gum
at my Commonwealth the teacher pretended to be
distracted by something in the hallway. My Commonwealth
had many questions about the curriculum, but she was
never called upon anytime that she raised her hand.

*

I have often been called a tempest, unruly,
difficult to manage, even though the song
on my skin is prescribed by most oncologists.

*

All these shanties you've erected
for the orphans of my Commonwealth
will outlast your broken treaties,
the melodrama of your tin cabarets.

★

He's followed Storni into the reefs
                    hoping perhaps
down there her toddlers
            will not be thrown
                        into kennels
            and told they must
represent themselves
      at the tribunal.

★

My Commonwealth is also
            your Commonwealth, yet
            you convince yourself she
owes you twenty dollars.

★

I took my Commonwealth to the garden, where
he turned the swans into rock stars. A couple
asked my Commonwealth to take their photograph
in front of the monk's bed. He made them
                  an ocean out of papier-mâché.

★

No maps exist that will lead you
      to my Commonwealth, though
      all her sidewalks are a map

to other Commonwealths
that also have no maps.

         ★

My Commonwealth speaks the language of fire ants
and labirintos azules. His blouses are tailor-made
to fit every version of himself. In all the gutters
he leaves guarachas that sprout into a local bar and grill.

         ★

In Buenos Aires there are three trees that survived
the bombing of Hiroshima. My Commonwealth
is like that, but she does not want to say she is like
that, as it would be a disservice to those who
actually survived the bomb. She is not
the survivor of atomic war, only a survivor
of colonialism. And racism. And sexism. And classism.
And marginalization. And molestation. And assault
by invisibility. And betrayal. And condescension.
And mockery. And accusations of altruism.

         ★

                It's true: though my Commonwealth
            is a certified lifeguard, she has
              an aversion to galleons.

         ★

Though they would never admit it, the vestibules
of Europe yearn for my Commonwealth. They hunt
whales and train their children to be tenors
that might sing my Commonwealth to shore.

*

          I call my Commonwealth
a terrace. He says, *Don't lie, my azaleas*
are pristine and there is room for a hammock,
                 yes. But I am just a balcony. A balcony
     more beautiful than any terrace, I reply.

*

I hope by now you understand that my Commonwealth is just
a metaphor, and that the use of *my* is not intended to claim
possession of them. Perhaps if I could speak the language of my
Commonwealth I'd know of a word better than *my* to use
when I speak of them. To assign the possessive to them is really
just a clumsy attempt at signifying kinship. I am also theirs, see.
So please take *my* to mean "I am of." This is not to say, however,
we are somehow one and the same. Pues, we have romped across
meridians in rhythm, but my Commonwealth is their own source.

*

          Do not mock my Commonwealth and call him
          babe. He will spit in your soup if you test him.

*

Politicians never visit my Commonwealth.
Activists never visit my Commonwealth.
Scholars never visit my Commonwealth.
Neoliberal philanthropists never visit
my Commonwealth. But they all wield

monumental opinions about my Commonwealth,
even though some of them don't even know that
my Commonwealth is a Commonwealth, don't

know there was no playground or hospital here until
she petitioned the city at the end of the last century.

Now they all want my Commonwealth to install
storm windows on every floor, but my Commonwealth
insists the sea can take whatever it wants, says she
is not and will never be a tax haven. She will
not answer to a junta. My Commonwealth

says the tide has always been her paramour,
her parasol, her paradox shifting paradigms
like tectonic plates, her clock and silo since
before there was a before. She is not about
to dissolve this partnership for a governing board

that still thinks price tags are anything more
           than a lonely child's imaginary friend.

     ★

Que bella! Que triste! they say about my Commonwealth.
           To which he says, *Go to musical hell,*
as he winks and dives from the pier.

     ★

           She fixes radios on the side, and paints summer
           onto stripped Peugeots. Her teasing ripens oranges
           and she keeps the street corners warm with her
           bandoneon. Public works always removes her
           mosaics from the city plazas, so she invents her
           own plazas to commemorate the missing ones.
           She gives them names like *Plaza of the Corn Mistress*
           and visits them in rotation to stage plays with her
           amigxs, theater to see for when one cannot see.

*

The trade winds are sure to utter me.
Then I will open and you will open,
            and my Commonwealth
will shine back the stones we flung at his head.

*

When I speak of my Commonwealth I am not speaking
of a flat I have ever lived in. Nor am I speaking of a lover
who spurned me. When I speak of my Commonwealth

I speak of an Elsewhere that lives in my left kidney,
a cavity growing in a tooth that is still waiting to erupt.
To refer to my Commonwealth is to admit that I do not

want to come from where I come from, a fantasy that
I have the right to bathe in a lake too cold for my
complexion, it is to claim that no claim is ever valid.

*

            I gave you dragon fruit
            and it wasn't enough. Gave
                        you the clave and it
            wasn't enough. Gave you sofrito,
                        Sotomayor, Chita
                  Rivera, and it wasn't enough.
      Gave you the guayabera and *Mendez*
                        v. Westminster
            and it wasn't enough. Gave you the stent
            and the hammock and it wasn't enough.
                  I gave you another way
                              to read the world
                  and it wasn't enough. You

                              accepted all this
from me and still you wanted
the credit.

    ★

Siempre limpiando. Siempre limpiando los Vidrios Ingleses.

    ★★★

The Satyricon of Maxwell Demon
(Cento for David Jones)

Ice on the cages. Ray guns in the market square. Eye peep space
ripples, abandon the stream. Precisely like puckering urchins who
grumble at gold. Not a hunky scientist drinking stardust and venom,
but every spider knows all things begin and end in a flotsam
of shampoo and five years of crying. Panther princess played sane

to my surrogate lips. Pin a scandal to my spangled silhouette.
Scars that can't be seen diamond every faux pas that mangles
my mind. Young boogaloo king wails *The wrong impression would
not be the wrong impression in the slightest.* My station is swollen,
my only interest is energy. I'm a saint abroad in low-flying sobriety.

Darling self-denial, the heroes in your hair are wasted and sunk
in a tangle of garlands. Like a lodger swimming with dolphins,
I saw you through a monster of rooms and suffragette imps slithering,
a standing cinema sweet-talking the cavemen, purring *Let's stab
the idiot questions tonight. Let me disappear in his Eldorado.* I've

got a stubborn impulse to be more than human. Slide down
with the gutter babies, face the perfumed machine with bubbles
and action. The banker's spleen has cracked. I was tin and he was
all brass noise and white stains. Now I'm just looking for treason
and spice wind charity. Outside the icon superior is throwing darts

at hologrammic girls in synthesis. Earthling in a psychodelicate dance
that breaks the sky in two. Bombs the hours from a laugh motel. Heathen
in satin and tat dredging out more idols than reality. No longer guided
by my fear of not being misunderstood, I get up and sleep off those
one-inch thoughts. I am what I play next. Nail me to a theater

of black fog, 'cause I'll never say anything nice again. How can I?

Cicatristes (Orchestral Version)

1. allegro

chaparral of silences
pliant wrist
mother bends the
clamps
when he is
the doctor pre
stitched across pupils
hooked to spires
his shredded

lung
pipes
gasp
confirmed
summons another
nosferatu
no reflection
flung
as mirage
colluding
scapula crumpled
he cannot say
recollections of
a nail
taped to
his mutiny
edges of starched men
obscuring
the wail

this child is
elastic his
right
the left
minced into
scribes lithium
his chassis
aspires
metacarpals
no one
plunges
no hint
capitulated

outbreak
in his comic

from collar he
unseen
on tongue

no he cannot
being mistaken for
fingers of
the most tender
tendons caught
now grated
his glint
before it escapes

slunk
contorted
fallow this father
no one notices
linoleum then
crosshair
flayed
to camouflage
with snark
seems to grasp
through sewage
or

a single inquiry
to his brow like
he casts
no heat
is content only
sung calluses
clavicle
as twigs no
gauzed
the head of
scotch
ends now mute is
the denticulate
wall of stucco
muffling

2. *adagio*

(Two decades of truncated visits and stifled self-exile to continents that could not pronounce your name will leave you sitting with them at dinner, your wife worried about your nausea, the color evacuating your cheeks, and you will be forced to insist it isn't the meal, don't send it back, and they will say to your wife, He acts like we used to beat him or something, *fooling only the barely touched salad.)*

⇒ Ebru (Testimonio)

Sunlit as you shoot free throws, their blunderbuss
howling from the sidelines stuffs you. This routine
plays out every afternoon. They call you faggot

so many times your ribs splinter into warring nations:
one half beginning to wonder if maybe you are,
the other side launching campaigns to convince

them (you) that it isn't true. In the border between,
a lone voice asks why this word is used to mean *less
than*. And so you absorb the slur, accepting

it as an exile legislated by concrete cockerels. Through
middle and high school you consent to their naming
you, nudging you to decamp for boys that circumvent

the Vaticans of masculinity: the garage, the ballpark.
You sense those othered boys are somehow braver.
They live uncloaked as a palette of sci-fi serials, show

tunes, drag cosplay soirees. Those boys, undaunted
by their own epicene epicenters, turn their abrasions
into fulgent monuments they charge the unfledged

to witness. You kiss a few of those boys, if only
to see whether the courtside pejoratives rammed
into you were postulate, but also because you

hope their gloss of lithe wit might bond to your
upper lip and remodel you into an alcazar
glimmering above the cloudswarm. With one boy

you venture to bow, posing as mirrored pachyderms,
but when you fumble to clutch his bole no torch
kindles you, and you find that you cannot drape

yourself with the title the ballers cast upon you.
Nonetheless, their tribe adopts you, although you
are not, like them, a bolide. They teach you how

to mold your scars into plumage and cutlass.
For this grace, as tribute, you vow to shoulder
their foundation and wings across any canyon

should they tire. You will hold their hands
to form a truss with them anytime they
have the need or yearning to stop traffic.

On Scarification (Ars Poetica)

The foot   is sharpened
by the road,   memory
          sharpened by longing.
Oak is carved into a double
                reed that sharpens
mourning into a monastery.
          Skin is sharpened
by a glance.   The eye

shears potential from marble.
          The impossible question
is a laceration,   a penumbra cast
                over a lake of clipped ivy.
The confession is sharpened
          by an unexpected
pause.   The child
is sharpened by scorn,

the tongue is sharpened
          by the book.   The book
is a vivisection of flowering
debacles.   Friction
          thins the bounty, cleaving
the crowd into a tarred path.
          The path is a blade
smelted from fear,   a razor polishing

          bristly cheeks until the skin
bears luster.   Atrocity is sharpened
          by its erasure from the plaza
of its birth.   The loss is etched
          into the spine of the family
until shank becomes trestle. Light
is sharpened by sorrow,   sorrow
                by solitude.

                    Each incision becomes
              a cay logged and registered,
                    another border
to be defended.   The edge
of all things dulls with the incursion
              of luxury, a shift in angle
whittles blockades down to gaunt
totems.   Every breath is a strop.

➤ *The Skin I Live In* (dir. Pedro Almodóvar, 2011)

I, cinder. I, skein etched with redolent scalpel. I am your son
recast as very lady. I, too, am kindling. My full lashes the wick
lit by thirst for a doting cheek. This denuding of the limbs
has flooded me with the conviction that the monster to fear
is man, a nebbish critter born gnarled and excoriated, a lewd
and feral interloper. Incarcerated in an ice chamber of sterile

forceps, I have emerged as an adipose palace ready to admit
that woman is more than garnish, more than a garish affidavit
granting license to prod a wanton itch. I, designer coquette
dismantled, resewn to receive the leer. I, freakvenus retuning
to rebuff the despot's advances. My hide shipped from Milan

and fashioned into a temple of sighs by a savant assailant.
I, vascular simulacrum, vessel sculpted to lure what I once
throbbed to possess. Shanked. I am left to roam as pruned
lymph nodes, scion of Frankenfranco. I, refuse spruced up

to operate as winking ornament. I decline this appointment
to the position of duvet. I clip the claw that wields the fetish
needle. I, liger, lithe glam liege, dissimulated masculine.

I slash the walls of this burette, convert into a rebel bauble
on the lam, and augment my spikelet until I live polyvalent.

Capsized. Revised. Abscinded from binaries. I ripen into total.

Areyto for the Shipwrecked: LatinX the Unknown

after Tracie Morris

If you dice it, it don't split. It
swells. Glows. Grows a spine of bass. Lines
halved by throat of the hive. Struck. Brine
of riled goats amped for lounge acts, lit
like post-pop flash mobs. It don't split
if you shear it. It dons hooves, fruits
lungs and surfs crowds. Sourced, sung in mute
tones of skin as drum. As stem, cell
blocked. Veins rich with bronze ore to smelt
ribs. As brass. As scorched tongue. As root

hacked. Like code. Blip spliced with stone. Sly
glitch trip. Synth blissed. A mist of why.
A mouth of light in molt. Pumped blood
as bolt. Not cut, but sighed through wood,
wind whirled as world. A gall bled dry
by seers suited in bytes. But don't push,
don't force. A heart is not a hushed
clock. Wise. A cracked act or hip crown.
This bi, a myth. Sliced, it's whole ground.
Split, it's a bridge of breath. Bright blush.

⇶ Ceraunoscope Vitae

The pop star googles herself and stumbles
                                onto a letter she wrote in kindergarten
                to her first crush. The boy grew up to be
a financial analyst who collects minor league hockey
                                     mascots. The pop star wears
                a wasp's nest to their high school reunion.

In preparation for his next world tour he is teaching
                        himself to resurrect glaciers.
            He plans to wear a candy
dispenser as a halter top during the encores
                            and waltz with a manatee
                in heat for the live webcast.

At press conferences she answers
                    all questions from journalists
            with a ham sandwich to the groin
while demurring into their tape recorders
                        that music is meant to be
            seen and not heard.

Before the premiere of her latest video,
                        she engages in epistemological debates
           with her emu-shaped swimming pool.
They agree this meaningless masquerade is just so
                        indelibly meaningful. To prove
           her virtuosity the pop star plays Chopin

using an MRI machine. During rehearsals he starves
                      himself by eating unborn unicorns,
           wipes his runny nose on the lesser-
known works of Jasper Johns.
                        In her stage dreams she pleads
           with a cyber-sylph to make her a real

live boy. Her favorite color is the sound
                         of a moped stalling. His favorite
              hobby is devising new ways to look
bored on the tour bus. At record release parties
                              she directs unpaid interns
              to re-create the Peloponnesian War

while she slaps a carp in the head with moldy shower curtains.
                    This year the Academy will present
              him with a lifetime achievement award
for all the songs he has refused to compose.
                         The pop star is now ghostwriting
              her own unauthorized autobiography

where she pretends to be strung out, unloved,
                         and now cancer-free. Her fans
              must set fire to the nearest mobile
communications retail outlet in order to get their own copy.
                         As an act of charity, he promises
              to shake martinis for all the orphaned hedgehogs

of the world. In the final chapter of their career, the pop star
                         revisits each of their veneers, then retires
              to live as a recipe for peach cobbler and professor
of paleontology. They have one blue eye, one green eye, one
                         owl eye, one winged eye, and one eye
              that has no opinion on the subject.

<Latin/X/futurist> <ElectriCode/X/otica>

@

sneezed quantum mermaid worship
wereships split atom atonally beneath
full moon river queens rolling Quixote

@

Drexciyan colony blasts HIJOS symphonic
colonic scratch wipe infovis santero rite
veil Hadron bachata metropole reformat

@

shock professors rock the cosplay thunder
isotope soda scriptures suture sculpture
Horus fashion resistance selfie stigmata

@

sail the string theory mangú carcass down
Xingu into crevice of sartorial dub genome
diamond squire wax ineffable germ fete

@

hyper-cabasa quark hoagie abducted in vitro
from qullqa blockbuster scratches niche bomb
boogie splice Quechua con sacerdotal metadata

@

bilingual electro-cult supplicates gray matter
quipu slang Boolean shastra breeds bio dope
fiduciary cougar coups in xenofunk mastaba

@

dame la vaca De La Vega diaspora junkie
neo-pseudo-proto-tele path Caribe nerd
punk proxy server femme mythos in furs

@

machine snot lathering ceiba hangover
skin grammar phone iPad ipecac Darth
Pinochet Faraday caged in cyber-calabash

@

perplexed helix exodus to digi-cairn of lapis
lazuli virtue de virtual value in post-post-post
blood nova upgrade in nanopool wild style

@

Toltech Boom de oro invokes Titan Rain
blackboxing modinhas to thump stump
Memex corregidors with superflare Zafa

@

ACT FIVE

"... excavating the explosion ..."

Laura Solórzano

PROMESA (HR 4900)

Song to ward off venture capitalists.

The tinto shipped
from our ancestors in Galicia
  flirts unabashedly with giggling hens
on the veranda. Tio Frank
    is praying to his pipe, the smoke
      cradles his bajo sexto
as he croons, conjuring the flota

    that dislocated us from the last
century. Junior rocks the ricochet
  like a sorcerer of Brownian
motion. He is a garrison perched
    across the ping-pong table
      like an eight-limbed
colossus. In the kitchen, cards

    are slapped like sinvergüenzas
round after round in an endless
  game of Texas Hold 'Em that holds
the cousins hostage. The winner
    is never the sucker
      with the ace, the winner
is he who talks shit with Fidel's

    fuerza bruta, an eight-hour
fusillade of slick digs and relentless
  boasts. Beside them abuelita
plays Zatoichi with the lechón
    asado, ropa vieja is swallowed
      by vagrant cangrejo
and bored nieces running

    on fumes from chasing
the dog around the chicken coops.
  This party was supposed to evanesce

long before sunup, but the coquito
                    is still spilling, the tías
                              still stalking the counter-
          rhythms of the timbale like Bolívar

across the Andes. The road
at the end of the driveway is shrapnel,
          the privatized water too steep
for our pockets, but we got tariffs
                    on this tanned euphoria
                              so no vulture
          funds can raid and strip

                    the assets from our
digames, our 'chachos, our
          oyes, our claros, our dales, our
'manos, our oites, our carajos,
                    our negritos, our vayas,
our banditos,
          our pa que tu lo sepas!

(whiteboard don't work) (closet where emiliano) (keeps his project)
(on sea) (pollution won't shut) (fatoumata learns to find) (square roots)
(on three-legged desk) (she answers adhan) (daily at lunch) (kaylani
conjugates verbs) (in her building's stairwell) (shares her room with
four siblings) (ac) (don't work) (bookshelves) (arid) (like arica) (adds
lianabelle) (yadira gashes her elbow) (no nurse on staff) (assistant
super drops by) (to order) (more lockdown drills) (there's gum stuck
in sharpener) (marifer shouts she's doing her research) (on policarpa)
(señora santiago affirms) (state exam) (judas cradle) (prep periods)
(chupacabra sightings) (we agree) (city budget be) (playing chimera)
(silviano has refused to speak english) (during english) (is teaching
himself to code) (bet) (shymel wonders why) (bars on our windows)
(be looking like) (rottweiler's) (rotting teeth) (white) (board don't)
(i got frisked here at) (work) (again) (metal detectors) (at the front)
(so(b)rash) (hoggish) (guard alleges he) (confiscates) (for real like)
(two hundred knives a week) (mr. moss tore his acl) (working out)
(still shows up early) (because) (his kids need to see he's got their)
(back) (board in gym) (cracked) (my back) (faulty transmission) (got
six periods to teach) (on two hours sleep) (no lie) (across the hall)
(white) (colleague calls) (sherlyn little) (thug) (pit bull) (another has)
(students marching) (across their classmates' spines) (as her slavery)
(lesson) (true story) (zuleyka confides) (that if our school were like)
(disney's high school musical she'd always want to be) (here) (on)
(board) (kelvin writes) (*inside my heart is an armadillo*) (jaelis writes)
(*men treat women's bodies like*) (*spain colonizing quisqueya*) (dariel wants
to know) (if i were a moon of jupiter) (which one would i be?)

☞ Ofrenda for Tom the Janitor

Tom, your name should grace the halls of every capitol building.
Your belt buckle larger than the blue Googie façade of a Las Vegas
casino, slung higher than the peaks of the Pyrenees, must be

bowed to by all who have ever gnawed on a bar of chocolate
and tossed the nonbiodegradable wrapper onto the scuffed tiles
for you to collect with a pincer and rubber gloves. If no one else

will sing for you, Tom, I will. I will carry your name in my briefcase,
to be called upon whenever a sink is clogged and those who deem
themselves above skin-hardening work will ignore it and shirk

the blame. Because you are the history of adolescent
irresponsibility. Your method of sopping up leaks
and leaving no trace may not be understood by the sloths

who created the reason for your employment, but without
your shrugged efforts every classroom would resemble
a landfill. For no man has ever scraped gum off

the undercarriage of a rusted desk with such dignity.
Spilled applesauce and mashed potatoes are at your
mercy. Cadaverous rodents are cleansed from behind

the bleachers of the gymnasium, you eradicate the viscous
dross of nauseated sophomores without even a nod of thanks.
Tom, with a paunch like a cast-iron stove and hair receding

like coastal banks, old leather shoes clomping through unkempt
stairwells. I will speak of you and your Fridays shot standing
at bus stations clad in outdated navy suits. I will tell them that

their life without you would be a cesspool, a sump, a morass
of pencil shavings and gutted calculators. As they drown
in their own detritus, I promise they will sing of you then.

➤ All the Mexicos

Fox News reported that the president is threatening to cut off aid to "three Mexican countries."

I want to live in all the Mexicos. The Mexico of Bolaño's nostalgic
fantasia. The Mexico where Eliécer Gaitán served up his allocutions.
Somewhere I won't be interrogated for taking a sick day. Where my

neighbor stops by to bring me caldo. I'll live in any Mexico. The Mexico
Rugama and Gioconda Belli called home. Or even one of the Mexicos
where everyone speaks French Creole. Any Mexico will do. So long

as I don't lose any more digits to these arctic gales. My lover once told
me of a Mexico where there are no advertisements and you'd swear
the café was brewed in gold. Sign me up for that Mexico. How about

the Mexico where Romero delivered his last sermon? Give me the ceiba
trees or dunes of the pampas, the cane fields of the Mexico that bred
my parents. My ankles are swelling from the sulfuric acid in these streets.

And if I'm going to be underpaid anyway, then why not take my coins to
the Mexico that houses the canal or one of the Mexicos the Orinoco runs
through. I'll set up shop in any Mexico that will have me, so long as I can

weep on plots of earth that can say *I'm so proud of you, mijo.* So ship
me to Ana Cristina Cesar's Mexico that also longs for the perhaps.
Box me up and leave me in Vallejo's Mexico with its startling volcanoes

of repentance. Give me all the Mexicos of the hemisphere, pistol-
whipped by United Fruit and still making wisecracks. I'll take root
in any Mexico that knows the difference between the gutter and stars.

⇒ On Privilege (Seigniorage)

On January 15, 2018, board members of the Oconomowoc Area School District in Wisconsin ordered the superintendent to not allow activities and discussions on the topic of social privilege in classrooms.

My skin is a privilege. Except when the human resources office eavesdrops on my abuelo's dialect. Or when I wake up in the baldest hour of night tormented by the ghost tendrils of my overseer uncle strangling my machetero uncle who refused to cut any more cane. My sex is a privilege, but only at awards ceremonies and job interviews. And in classrooms. Or standing in line. Or at departmental meetings and transatlantic flights. Okay, everywhere. But this beast bites back when I've occupied another night cauterizing the lacerations that others of my sex have carved into my wife with their scimitar of privilege. Then my privilege is a damaged retina and a heart with one chamber too few, a limp I never asked the central office to send me. To be born in this city is a privilege. But only as long as there is electricity, for without power this metropolis is just a cave of helpless gnats who do not know how to sew or start their own fires. To be born in this country, or so I've been told, is also a privilege, only not so much on the other end of transatlantic flights. I have worn the spit of natives who wanted me to know that I was not invited. And it is a privilege to sit in a Michelin-rated restaurant, to call down to the concierge for fresh towels. These are all privileges born from my education. Yes, education is a privilege, although you wouldn't know it by listening to the pundits on the evening news. Education is a privilege, except that here it always comes packaged in the bond-slavery of loans. Education, yes, is a privilege, but it is also a sixty-mile-high electrified fence that cloisters me from my students, who were raised in a borough with no bookstores or lymphoma-free vegetables. My privilege is so privileged that I find it hard to see how their Galaxy phones are a necessity but a home library is not. I should consider my health to be a privilege as well. Prostate exams have become a luxury I procrastinate. My house is laden with protein and apple cider vinegar. I have an allergist on speed dial. I am able to opt out of chain-food manslaughter, abstain from GMOs as an act of protest. My work allows me this privilege. Having work is a privilege, except that the aforementioned bond-slavery of loans affixed to my education ensures that I will work so much my health will all too soon be at risk. Still, work is a privilege.

I've known hunger, and it comes with no privilege. My line of work
has kept my hands unscarred and tender, though periodically dried
out from chalk, my nails filed and shining, unlike the nails of my
father, which are a charred battleground of diesel grease and drill bit
residue, his fingertips cracked like winter asphalt. Actuaries informed
him that his work will shave ten years off his life. All the welding it
required threatens to steal his eyesight. My eyes are a privilege,
as are the glasses that aid them. Glasses and fathers are a privilege.
I have students who lack and need both. I suppose light and warmth
are now privileges, though they probably shouldn't be. But my sweater
from H&M is clearly a privilege sewn where child labor laws are fantasy.
A privilege that I own sweaters, and a chest full of socks, and shoes
for each day of the week, and the online service that delivers me
packages containing limited-press vinyl records, and the subway line
that takes me to work for less than three dollars, and the bridge I cross
to get to the train, and the café where I stop for a macchiato, the paper
I read while drinking it. It's all a privilege. A privilege to not have to think
of all the human energy invested in making sure I arrive and return safely
to an unmade bed and hot shower, and a floor. Yes, the floor in my flat
is even a privilege. In southern Turkey, I once stayed in a home without
one. The ground in that abode was undoubtedly cleaner than the ceramic
tiles in my kitchen. Ceramic tiles are a privilege. Being able to travel to
Turkey is a privilege. It's clear now that travel and floors are privileges.
And appliances. Kitchens, too, are a privilege. Ask any New Yorker.
And let's not forget about plumbing, the ultimate privilege. It's all
a shimmering and turgid carnival of privilege, if only because we have
agreed that some people deserve these things while others do not.
There are men bestowed with the job of devising calculations to assign
these privileges, men who are privileged with scripting policies that
determine what each of us is worth. These policies are both cause
and effect of privilege. It absolves the authors, and us, of having
to haul pity and guilt around in our satchels, providing us the privilege
of pretending our privilege is a burden. My privilege, both crown

and crutch, is an unearned spoil. It spoils the meal, spoils offspring, spreads willful blindness, spills oil into the Gulf of Mexico. To be aware of this is a privilege, a cirrocumulus of shame above my veranda. My privilege is a coltan skull, product of machines that proliferate lack. This machine of lack, mute and merciless godfather of all privilege.

L'Eclisse (dir. Michelangelo Antonioni, 1962)

Prattle. Thrum of the exchange floor
swelters and swells the walls excommunicating
double-breasted swindlers from the pharmacy. Monica

Vitti swaggers in, inoculated and far too lethargic
to be undone. Her gaze besieges Alain
Delon and his crystalline chin carved by Giotto.

He's roaring like a toreador, toying
with the pendulum of net losses and gains. She sidles,
winks, draws him out from the dross

and into a world forever under
construction: half-built manors encroached by half-
built offices. Together they wade, startled

by the immensity of verandas that cannot hold
the weight of their trove of ribald absences.
This dalliance acts as respite. In her

his tyranny of irrational equations is subdued. In him
she procures an accomplice to instigate
a courtship with indecision. Among the strewn

relics of an empire only the young wish to forget,
they shade themselves in a charade, an elongated
dime store romance made soggy

by tossed bathwater, promising to spend tomorrow
and tomorrow in the plush embrace
of the other, until tomorrow rears its cavalier head, bringing

them only a landscape of rusty buckets, deserted
cafés, drunken motors plucked from the sea, termites
converging upon the capitol steps, an icy arson they agree

to ignore should it ever beg them to stay.

Punk Aubade for Hardcore Chica

for Grisel, and a response to Pablo Neruda's "I Like for You to Be Still"

I like for you to be clamorous: it is as though you were a stack
of Marshall amps in a concert hall. My listless mind is quickened

by your dulcet caterwauls. It seems as though your irises radiate
as filtered Fresnels rousing me from a disquiet repose. You do not

emerge from me, you emerge sovereign from your own collaged
cocoon of glitter and leather jackets. Why would I ever want you still

and distant? For I tingle when you flutterswirl, composing etudes
out of cabaret camp and critical race theory. I do not want you absent

and Stepford amenable, or remote like an ingenue with clenched lip
and heart awaiting rescue. I want you as you are: as boisterous

as a campus sit-in. When I talk to you, do not be silent. Silence me
with the B-side bravado of your Jello Biafra badinage. Supinate me

with the voltage of your steel-toed boots, your unbridled scrutiny
of gender inequality. I like for you to be blustering, unapologetic,

an ebullient tempest of community projects and brandy-infused
mosh pits. No. You are not like my soul. You are like your soul:

the Cramps blasting through an Argento giallo populated by Araki
freaks. I like for you to be zoetic: it is as though you are nightclub

subwoofers demolishing every sham throne with your meticulous
thunder. I like for you to be not as I like, but as you are: all rose

skull ink cavorting through beer-soaked dance halls, rambunctious
as an Archangel Blue, the convivial Grand Dame doing the Time Warp

at an end of the world fiesta. It is as though you were amaranthine
and one blustering word from you, one X-ray smirk, is not enough.

NSFW Poem for Dirty Minds

Dithering in the steam of dawn I feel your toes
searching for mine. It is Sunday and the mochi

we ate with last night's dinner has lingered
in the crevices between our teeth. I promised

you I'd clean out the second closet, and your
mother needs help finding a new caretaker

for your father. The bills need to be mailed and we
are out of cat litter so a shower seems in order,

but last night you offered to serve hot
pancakes this morning and I am friskier when

the coffee is slow-pour, so we don't leave
the house until noon. The line at the store

is too long, causing my neck to itch. You tickle
my elbow and pull at my ears until my heart

downshifts from tremor to purr. We have
trouble finding a new set of towels that match

the bathroom, and your mother is being
stubborn about who she lets in to clean

the apartment. Gangling, I jostle as a skeleton
clown in the produce section, and you pretend

to be embarrassed, though now you brush
closer to me when you place the salmon

in our cart. We ask ourselves if we have too many
snacks. And I know it would make you happy

if we got the car washed, so I make the detour,
if only to watch you become five again, your

eyes turning into lava lamps as you gaze
at the suds huddled on the windshield, your

wool hat framing you with a crown of rouge.
Now you are hungry and my longing for

a macchiato has become a glacier, and we
are feeling naughty, so we order macaroons

and chat too long about the books we want
to read next summer, until you say something

cobblestone-in-autumn pretty about how
proud you are of your former student who

just got accepted into graduate school,
and now I want to get you home before

the caffeine wears off, so I demand the check,
and we've barely closed the front door when

the phone rings. It's your mother still at war
with her sadness. I unload the car and clip

the cat's nails and your Celia Cruz cadence
calms all listeners across two states, until

I finally get you out of your shoes and onto
your belly, splayed across the couch, to punish

the knots on your shoulder that plague you.
You groan as the pain diffuses into twinkles

of relief. You turn over and whisper *thank you*.
And we lay hand to foot, cradling the knees

of the other, clutching to prolong the arrival
of the small hours. I rise with a grunt to pour

two thumbs of rye. We clink glasses, place them
on end tables. The television murmurs, but we

cannot seem to remember who turned it on.
It flickers with jealousy as we stare at each other

like two ancient pelicans perched on a buoy. We
mime the scratching of boxed kittens. Ossified

and aching, our snoring synchronizes. Laundry
is still in the dryer, the kitchen light left on.

⟿ Areytos for the Shipwrecked:

The Case for Spanglish

Because a corazón is more resilient than a heart. Because when
my abuelo's spleen ruptured right there on Queens Boulevard
he yanked himself up with nothing but smog to hold onto and walked
home fifteen blocks before eventually collapsing on the bathroom
floor. That takes babilla. Simple courage won't do. Because songs
are nice but a canción bathes inside the veins. The dankdim nightclub
lounges of my youth gave me confidence, it's true, but only Lavoe's
rooster calls are able to resurrect the dead, only Celia's "azúcar!"
incites warring tribes to fall in love. Because an abrazo can shield you
from famine and flame. A hug lacks that kind of sorcery. Because
bochinche is both science and art. It can turn men into rats
and spread through the respiratory system like a viral infection.
Gossip is simply no match for bochinche. Because el sol is spirit,
sun is its child. Because árboles are monasteries for the lost, while
men don't think twice about felling trees. Because díos inspires
humility like no god can. Because vida blossoms from the mouth
like a fulgent garden, while life is merely the title of a game,

a syllable in search of a hyphen.

Quenepas

everywhere. Slung across church
pews. Poking out from the light
fixtures in a panadería. Quenepas
multiplying like tribbles, their vines
strangling the statue of a surfer
in the town square. Erupting
like a volcano of syrupy pulp
drowning the arraigned hedge
fund managers that have infested
these tropics. Quenepas fueling
the hens, their nectar acting as glue
for dioramas of the Ponce Massacre
students craft for their history
classes. Quenepas squirting
into the pupils of a petulant
commander in chief reaching
to fondle a leatherback turtle.
Quenepas. Their pits choking
cryptocurrency conquistadors,
suffocating them as quenepa
juice froths from their nostrils
and ears. Quenepas everywhere.
In the carcasses of trapiches
and under the hoods of used
Volvos. Quenepas strung
like Christmas lights from El Faro
to the Tower of Yuisa. Quenepas.
Dipping to La India. Sugarseed.
Bohique pendant. Waterstar.
Tan dulce tapestry. Adorning
a million canicules. Entiendes?

NOTES

1. *On Battling (Baltimore Strut)*: This poem is inspired by Dimitri Reeves. After Freddie Gray was found dead in police custody in Baltimore in April 2015, protests arose throughout the city. During the protests, as police presence grew and their reactions to the protesters became more aggressive, Reeves popped up at numerous locations where the tensions had escalated and proceeded to dance on top of trucks, in front of SWAT team barricades—even dancing before an armored police carrier, as this poem alludes to. *Featherglide*, *thunderclap*, and *toprock* are the names of dance moves.

2. *Days of Being Wild*, *Sleep Dealer*, *Once Upon a Time in Anatolia*, *The Skin I Live In*, and *L'Eclisse* are all cinephrastic poems of films that bear the same title. Cinephrastic poems are essentially ekphrastic poems, but instead of responding to paintings, they respond to films.

3. *Human Instamatic* takes its title from a painting by Martin Wong. In Puerto Rico, pitorro is what is known as moonshine, or homemade alcohol.

4. *"Puerto Rico Is Burning Its Dead"* is titled after a headline taken from a news article in *BuzzFeed* on the aftermath of Hurricane Maria. The full title of the article is "Puerto Rico Is Burning Its Dead, and We May Never Know How Many People the Hurricane Really Killed," and it was written by Nidhi Prakash. Elihu Root was President Theodore Roosevelt's secretary of state. Root was prominent in shaping the Unites States' colonial policy.

5. *Areyto for the Shipwrecked: Lost Articles*: The poem is an erasure of a piece of the Jones Act, from the article titled "Sec. 6. Sale to Aliens." It is this clause from the Jones Act that kept other countries from being able to send relief supplies to Puerto Rico after the hurricane. Under the act, only ships flying U.S. flags can dock in Puerto Rico's ports. The president initially

refused to temporarily waive the act, waiting several days after the hurricane before finally agreeing to do so.

6. *Latinxorcismos: Semiotic Study of the Gringo Horror Film (Required Reading)*: This poem draws conceptually from theories of Dr. Grisel Y. Acosta on xenophobia and horror films. An Afro-Latinx scholar and author, and avid horror film fan, Dr. Acosta has observed that many of these films use the narrative structure of a foreign person or species entering (read: invading) a community or a group of protagonists visiting (read: invading) a space only to be tortured and then killed by some supernatural force. The films using either of these structures seem to subtly, or sometimes not so subtly, present the source of horror in the film as an entity that is clearly not white, which is to say the entity is not committed to whiteness. They are designed as monsters that do not speak English (usually they are just a screeching creature or sometimes mute), often brown or dark in hue, and they are rarely given their own back stories that might allow the viewer to identify with them, occluding any space for empathy toward the film's monster. Moreover, so many of these films take place in big houses where property—territory—becomes central to the conflict, taking the colonizer's position of defending land that they have stolen and now claim as their own. Dr. Acosta has said that this is why, when watching these films, she tends to identify with the monster rather than the protagonists. Read through the lens of the Latinx experience, one can't help but notice how, in the real world, nonwhite people of the Americas are very much demonized and painted as a threat to the notion of the nice American (read: white) family. Considering the proliferation of such films in the horror genre and how they run parallel to the transmission of anti-Latinx rhetoric in the public sphere in the U.S., it seems like something more than coincidence that the story lines created by the film/policy-maker in both of these arenas are built up around the same attitudes and symbolism. My aim with this poem was to play with the genre's familiar tropes and imagery to build an extended metaphor that illustrates Dr. Acosta's theory of the horror genre as an anti-Latinx propaganda delivery system.

7. Sleep Dealer *(dir. Alex Rivera, 2008)*: A *coyote* is someone who is paid to smuggle people across the U.S.-Mexico border. A *maquila* is a factory that employs low-wage Mexican workers to manufacture raw materials and export them back to the U.S.

8. *"Give Me My Flowers While I Yet Live"* takes its title from the name of a painting by Trenton Doyle Hancock. The parenthetical quote at the end of the poem was written on one of his paintings.

9. *Nonstop from Fruitvale to Ursa Major: Ofrenda for Los Desaparecidos of the United States*: In Latin America, los desaparecidos are those who were victims of the "forced disappearances" by repressive state governments through methods of kidnapping, torture, detainment, and assassination. Nearly forty years after Argentina's Dirty War, where more than thirty thousand people were "disappeared," the U.S. is creating its own brand of "the disappeared" in the form of an ever-growing number of murders of black men and women committed by police officers without any subsequent punishment or legal consequence.

10. Once Upon a Time in Anatolia *(dir. Nuri Bilge Ceylan, 2011)*: *Hüzün* is a Turkish word for which there is no accurate translation, but in his book *Istanbul*, Orhan Pamuk describes it as a kind of melancholy, a deep emotional anguish that causes a person to be withdrawn. *Bir tanem* in Turkish means "sweetheart."

11. *Core Curriculum Standards: Parkland, Belmont, Marshall County, Aztec, Rancho Tehama, Townville, Marysville, Reynolds, Arapahoe, Sparks, Sandy Hook, Chardon, Nickel Mines, Platte Canyon, Red Lake, Rocori, Red Lion, Santana, Columbine, et al.*: Aguirre was a Spanish conquistador. In Taíno culture, Coaybay is the land of the dead.

12. *Insolvency*: A *guanín* is a charm or pendant that was typically worn by Taíno chiefs, signifying one's lineage and social status.

13. *Areyto for the Shipwrecked: Re/Vuelta: Conuco* is a Taíno word for "farm."

14. *Anthropomorphic Study of the Antilles:* In the Taíno religion, Guabancex is the goddess of storms. A caney is a shelter with palm leaves for a roof where tobacco is hung to dry, or a general covered work area in the villages of the Taínos, Caribes, and Arawaks. Bayamanaco is the Taíno god of fire. Sycorax is an unseen character in William Shakespeare's *The Tempest*. She is a witch and the mother of Caliban. The Milwaukee Deep is the deepest part of the Atlantic Ocean, located in the Caribbean. Kick 'Em Jenny is a submarine volcano located just south of Saint Vincent and the Grenadines.

15. *My Commonwealth*: Alfonsina Storni is an Argentine poet famous in her home country. She was known to have committed suicide by walking into the sea. Sonia Sotomayor is the first Latina Supreme Court justice. Chita Rivera is a Puerto Rican dancer and Broadway actress known for her performances in *Sweet Charity* and *West Side Story*. *Mendez v. Westminster* is the 1947 federal court case that challenged the forced segregation of Latino students into separate schools. This case set legal precedent that became essential in the famous *Brown v. Board of Education* case.

16. *The Satyricon of Maxwell Demon (Cento for David Jones)* was constructed using the following self-imposed rules: The poem is twenty-six lines long to represent the twenty-six original studio albums recorded by David Bowie. A word from the title of each of the twenty-six albums appears throughout the poem in chronological order of each album's release date. All the language in the poem is extracted from song lyrics written by David Bowie, quoted from lines delivered by David Bowie in a film, or quoted from Todd Haynes's fictional David Bowie–inspired biopic, *Velvet Goldmine*.

17. *Areyto for the Shipwrecked: LatinX the Unknown*: This poem is written in a poetic form developed in Puerto Rico known as the décima.

18. *<Latin/X/futurist> <ElectriCode/X/otica>*: Here is a mini-glossary of terms for the poem.

> **cabasa:** A small percussion instrument.
>
> **cairn:** A mound of rough stones.
>
> **calabash:** A kind of gourd, or a tree native to the Americas.
>
> **ceiba:** A genus of trees indigenous to the Caribbean and West Africa.
>
> **corregidor:** A local official in charge of a territory of the Spanish Empire.
>
> **Drexciya:** A house music duo from Detroit. They claimed their band was named for an underwater nation populated by unborn children of pregnant women who were tossed from slave ships.
>
> **infovis:** Shorthand for "information visualization." Used in the tech industry, it is the study of visual representations of abstract data.
>
> **mangú:** A dish that is popular with Dominicans and other Caribbean communities.
>
> **mastaba:** A type of Egyptian tomb.
>
> **Memex:** Data system concept created by Vannevar Bush intended to help people improve their lives by having access to massive amounts of information.
>
> **modinha:** A song style popular in Brazil and Portugal that is overly romantic or sentimental.
>
> **quipu:** From the Andean region, quipus are used to record mathematical data by using a series of knotted strings bound together.
>
> **qullqa:** During the Incan Empire, qullqa, or collcas, were storehouses set along roads.
>
> **shastra:** In Sanskrit, a text that serves as a manual or compendium.

superflare: Large explosions that occur on stars; they are much stronger than solar flares.

Toltec: Tribe of people in Mexico that preceded the Aztecs.

Xingu: Both a river in Brazil and the name of a tribe indigenous to Brazil.

Zafa: In the culture of the Dominican Republic and elsewhere in the Caribbean, a Zafa is the counter-spell to a curse.

19. *PROMESA (HR 4900):* The poem's title is also the name of the federal law that installed a financial oversight board in Puerto Rico (the Puerto Rico Oversight, Management, and Economic Stability Act). Known among Puerto Ricans as La Junta, this governing board has complete control over the island's economy and has been responsible for implementing a severe austerity policy that has shut down more than one hundred schools on the island; the board is also working to privatize most of Puerto Rico's public assets and resources.

20. *Ofrenda for Tom the Janitor:* An ofrenda is an altar made up of a collection of objects that is placed on display during the Mexican Day of the Dead celebration. The ofrenda is intended to honor and celebrate a person who has died.

21. *All the Mexicos* was written in response to a report on Fox News that referred to three different Latin American countries, with obviously different names, cultures, and histories, as "three Mexican countries." The poem makes reference to several iconic Latin American figures:

    Roberto Bolaño: A Chilean author known for his novel *The Savage Detectives*.

    Jorge Eliécer Gaitán: A Colombian political leader, known for the eloquence of his speeches, who was assassinated during his campaign to become elected president of Colombia.

    Leonel Rugama: A Nicaraguan poet who died fighting against the Somoza dictatorship at the age of twenty.

    Gioconda Belli: A Nicaraguan poet whose poems were known for confronting issues of sexism.

    Saint Romero: Óscar Romero was an archbishop in El Salvador who was assassinated for speaking out against his country's military dictatorship for their acts of mass murder and torture committed against their own citizens.

    Ana Cristina Cesar: A Brazilian poet who committed suicide by leaping from a window.

César Vallejo: A Peruvian poet and journalist. One of the most widely read poets in Latin America.

22. *Areytos for the Shipwrecked: The Case for Spanglish & Quenepas*: The Ponce Massacre took place on Palm Sunday, March 21, 1937, in the town of Ponce, Puerto Rico. Police opened fire on a crowd of peaceful protesters, resulting in the deaths of nineteen people, with more than two hundred others wounded. A *canicule* is a heat wave.

ACKNOWLEDGMENTS

I offer my most Boom for Real thanks to the editors of the following journals and anthologies for publishing versions of poems from this book.

Anomaly Literary Journal: "PROMESA (HR 4900)"

Barzakh: Early versions of sections from "Core Curriculum Standards" and "Fox & Foghorn"

BOAAT: "On Bombing"

The Breakbeat Poets, Vol. 4: LatiNext: "Areyto for the Shipwrecked: DREAMcatcher," "Areyto for the Shipwrecked: Lost Articles," "On Bombing," and "*Sleep Dealer* (dir. Alex Rivera, 2008)"

Chiricú Journal: "Areyto for the Shipwrecked: DREAMcatcher," "Human Instamatic," and "*Sleep Dealer* (dir. Alex Rivera, 2008)"

Cloud Rodeo: "*Days of Being Wild* (dir. Wong Kar-Wai, 1990)"

Codex: "Insolvency" and "The Unscathed"

Five Quarterly: "Reciprocal Aubade for My Scopophiliac"

Found Poetry Review: "The Satyricon of Maxwell Demon (Cento for David Jones)"

Glass: A Journal of Poetry: "Latinxorcismos: Semiotic Study of the Gringo Horror Film (Required Reading)"

Hawai'i Review: "On Battling (Baltimore Strut)" and "PROMESA (HR 4900)"

Huizache: "Areyto for the Shipwrecked: Re/Vuelta"

The Journal: "On Scarification (Ars Poetica)"

Kweli: "Areyto for the Shipwrecked: Re/Vuelta"

Ostrich Review: "Disco Ballistics"

Paterson Literary Review: "Ofrenda for Tom the Janitor"

Rattle: "All the Mexicos"

Shrew: "Core Curriculum Standards: Parkland, Belmont, Marshall County, Aztec, Rancho Tehama, Townville, Marysville, Reynolds, Arapahoe, Sparks, Sandy Hook, Chardon, Nickel Mines, Platte Canyon, Red Lake, Rocori, Red Lion, Santana, Columbine, et al."

SX Salon: "Anthropomorphic Study of the Antilles" and "Mutiny at the Elder Care Facility"

Split This Rock: "Nonstop from Fruitvale to Ursa Major: Ofrenda for Los Desaparecidos of the United States"

The Texas Review: "<Latin/X/futurist> <ElectriCode/X/otica>" and "Puerto Rico Is Burning Its Dead"

Washington Square Review: "Give Me My Flowers While I Yet Live"

I wish to send my deepest gratitude to mi vida, Dr. Grisel Y. Acosta, for . . . well, for everything. Thank you for sharing your genius and your love with me.

Shoutouts to the following organizations for supporting my work during the writing of this book:

The Center for Puerto Rican Studies, Hunter College, New York

The Cooper Union for the Advancement of Science and Art, New York

Dodge Poetry Festival, Morristown, New Jersey

DreamYard Project, Bronx, New York

Guild Literary Complex, Chicago

The Jack Kerouac School of Disembodied Poetics, Naropa University, Boulder, Colorado

The Latinx Writers Caucus, AWP

Letras Latinas

Libería La Sede, Buenos Aires, Argentina

The Macondo Foundation, San Antonio, Texas

Montclair Literary Festival, New Jersey

The Poetry Center, Passaic County Community College, Paterson, New Jersey

Poetry Society of America, New York

Poets & Writers, New York

Poets House, New York

Big shoutouts to Willie Perdomo. Without him y'all might not be holding this book right now. For real, though.

More shoutouts to Paul Slovak and the entire team at Penguin Random House. You handled my poems with such care, authority, and respect. I am grateful for all the support you gave and all the work you put into this book.

Even more shoutouts to Francisco Aragon, Rosebud Ben-Oni, Julia Berick, Sarah Browning, Dr. Norma Cantu, Marina Carreira, Ching-In Chen and Cassie, Natalie Diaz, Carolina Ebeid, David Flores, Roberto Carlos Garcia, Carmen Gimenez Smith, Cindy Goncalves, Rigoberto Gonzalez, Ellen Hagan, Janet Holmes, Rick Kearns, John Keene, Raina J. León, Ricardo Maldonado, Cynthia Manick, J. Michael Martinez, Maria Mazziotti Gillan, Ian McAllen, Kamilah Aisha Moon, Tracie Morris, Urayoán Noel, Cynthia Dewi Oka, Laura Pegram, Marcos Perearnau, Emmy Perez, Jeffrey Pethybridge, Ellen Placey Wadey, Andy Powell, Ruben Quesada, Carmen Rivera, Raquel Salas Rivera, Craig Santos Perez, Bryanna Tidmarsh, Candido Tirado, Michael VanCalbergh, Anne Waldman, and Renee Watson. Everyone here helped make this book possible by offering manuscript feedback, promoting my work on the page and in classrooms and on stages, getting me gigs, offering me much-needed affirmations, and simply being kind to me. Mil gracias to all of you, and to all those unnamed who have contributed to making my world just Stink of Wow!

Vincent Toro is a Puerto Rican poet, playwright, director, and educator. He is the author of *Stereo.Island.Mosaic.*, which was awarded the Poetry Society of America's Norma Farber First Book Award and the Sawtooth Poetry Prize. He is also the winner of the Spanish Repertory Theater's Nuestras Voces Playwriting Award, and is a former Poets House Emerging Poets Fellow and a New York Foundation for the Arts Poetry Fellow. His work has been published in dozens of magazines and journals, including *Washington Square Review, BOAAT, Rattle, Vinyl, The Acentos Review, The Buenos Aires Review*, and *Best American Experimental Writing 2015*.

GAROUS ABDOLMALEKIAN
Lean Against This Late Hour

PAIGE ACKERSON-KIELY
Dolefully, A Rampart Stands

JOHN ASHBERY
Selected Poems
Self-Portrait in a Convex
 Mirror

PAUL BEATTY
Joker, Joker, Deuce

JOSHUA BENNETT
The Sobbing School

TED BERRIGAN
The Sonnets

LAUREN BERRY
The Lifting Dress

JOE BONOMO
Installations

PHILIP BOOTH
Lifelines: Selected Poems
 1950–1999
Selves

JIM CARROLL
Fear of Dreaming: The
 Selected Poems
Living at the Movies
Void of Course

ALISON HAWTHORNE
DEMING
Genius Loci
Rope
Stairway to Heaven

CARL DENNIS
Another Reason
Callings
New and Selected Poems
 1974–2004
Night School
Practical Gods
Ranking the Wishes
Unknown Friends

DIANE DI PRIMA
Loba

STUART DISCHELL
Backwards Days
Dig Safe

STEPHEN DOBYNS
Velocities: New and Selected
 Poems: 1966–1992

EDWARD DORN
Way More West

ROGER FANNING
The Middle Ages

ADAM FOULDS
The Broken Word: An Epic
 Poem of the British Empire
 in Kenya, and the Mau Mau
 Uprising Against It

CARRIE FOUNTAIN
Burn Lake
Instant Winner

AMY GERSTLER
Dearest Creature
Ghost Girl
Medicine
Nerve Storm
Scattered at Sea

EUGENE GLORIA
Drivers at the Short-Time
 Motel
Hoodlum Birds
My Favorite Warlord
Sightseer in This Killing City

DEBORA GREGER
By Herself
Desert Fathers, Uranium
 Daughters
God
In Darwin's Room
Men, Women, and Ghosts
Western Art

TERRANCE HAYES
American Sonnets for My Past
 and Future Assassin
Hip Logic
How to Be Drawn
Lighthead
Wind in a Box

NATHAN HOKS
The Narrow Circle

ROBERT HUNTER
Sentinel and Other Poems

MARY KARR
Viper Rum

WILLIAM KECKLER
Sanskrit of the Body

JACK KEROUAC
Book of Blues
Book of Haikus
Book of Sketches

JOANNA KLINK
Circadian
Excerpts from a Secret
 Prophecy
The Nightfields
Raptus

JOANNE KYGER
As Ever: Selected Poems

ANN LAUTERBACH
Hum
If in Time: Selected Poems,
 1975–2000
On a Stair
Or to Begin Again
Spell
Under the Sign

CORINNE LEE
Plenty
Pyx

PHILLIS LEVIN
May Day
Mercury
Mr. Memory & Other Poems

PATRICIA LOCKWOOD
Motherland Fatherland
 Homelandsexuals

WILLIAM LOGAN
Macbeth in Venice
Madame X
Rift of Light
Strange Flesh
The Whispering Gallery

J. MICHAEL MARTINEZ
Museum of the Americas

ADRIAN MATEJKA
The Big Smoke
Map to the Stars
Mixology

MICHAEL MCCLURE
*Huge Dreams: San Francisco
    and Beat Poems*

ROSE MCLARNEY
Forage
Its Day Being Gone

DAVID MELTZER
*David's Copy: The Selected
    Poems of David Meltzer*

ROBERT MORGAN
Dark Energy
Terroir

CAROL MUSKE-DUKES
Blue Rose
*An Octave Above Thunder:
    New and Selected Poems*
Red Trousseau
Twin Cities

ALICE NOTLEY
Certain Magical Acts
Culture of One
The Descent of Alette
Disobedience
For the Ride
In the Pines
Mysteries of Small Houses

WILLIE PERDOMO
The Crazy Bunch
*The Essential Hits of Shorty
    Bon Bon*

DANIEL POPPICK
Fear of Description

LIA PURPURA
*It Shouldn't Have Been
    Beautiful*

LAWRENCE RAAB
The History of Forgetting
*Visible Signs: New and
    Selected Poems*

BARBARA RAS
The Last Skin
One Hidden Stuff

MICHAEL ROBBINS
Alien vs. Predator
The Second Sex

PATTIANN ROGERS
Generations
Holy Heathen Rhapsody
Quickening Fields
Wayfare

SAM SAX
Madness

ROBYN SCHIFF
A Woman of Property

WILLIAM STOBB
Absentia
Nervous Systems

TRYFON TOLIDES
*An Almost Pure Empty
    Walking*

VINCENT TORO
Tertulia

SARAH VAP
Viability

ANNE WALDMAN
Gossamurmur
Kill or Cure
Manatee/Humanity
Trickster Feminism

JAMES WELCH
Riding the Earthboy 40

PHILIP WHALEN
Overtime: Selected Poems

ROBERT WRIGLEY
*Anatomy of Melancholy and
    Other Poems*
Beautiful Country
Box
*Earthly Meditations: New and
    Selected Poems*
Lives of the Animals
Reign of Snakes

MARK YAKICH
*The Importance of Peeling
    Potatoes in Ukraine*
Spiritual Exercises
*Unrelated Individuals
    Forming a Group Waiting
    to Cross*